RESEARCH LIBRARY
OF
COLONIAL AMERICANA

**RESEARCH LIBRARY
OF
COLONIAL AMERICANA**

General Editor
RICHARD C. ROBEY
Columbia University

Advisory Editors
JACK P. GREENE
Johns Hopkins University

EDMUND S. MORGAN
Yale University

ALDEN T. VAUGHAN
Columbia University

AN Hiſtorical Account

OF THE
Riſe and Growth of the
Weſt-INDIA COLLONIES

[Sir Dalby Thomas]

ARNO PRESS
A New York Times Company
New York – 1972

Robert Manning Strozier Library

JUN 29 1978

Tallahassee, Florida

Reprint Edition 1972 by Arno Press Inc.

Reprinted from a microfilm copy furnished by
Columbia University Library

LC# 75-141095
ISBN 0-405-03300-1

Research Library of Colonial Americana
ISBN for complete set: 0-405-03270-6
See last pages of this volume for titles.

Manufactured in the United States of America

Publisher's Note: This volume was reprinted
from the best available copy.

AN Historical Account

OF THE

Rise and Growth of the

West-INDIA COLLONIES,

And of the Great Advantages they are to *England*, in respect to Trade.

Licenced According to Order.

LONDON,

Printed for *Jo* Hindmarsh at the Golden-Ball, over against the Royal-Exchange. 1690.

To my much Honoured Friend Sir Robert Davers,

Baronet, and to the rest of the Gentlemen Interested and Concern'd in the

West-INDIES.

Gentlemen,

THe following Treatise was occasion'd by the great and Just Complaints made by you, of the Additional duty that was laid upon your Product, and fell upon your Labour and Industry, tho' design'd by the Parliament to have been paid by the Consumptioner; at that time the Inventions of most Men were at work (especially those that had any dealing with you, and a sense of your sufferings) to contrive a Method whereby relief might have been given to you that are the best Employ'd hands for the Enriching and supporting this Nation.

After much time had been spent, in endeavouring the taking off the Duty, and found that no Arguments were prevalent, and almost all People despairing of Relief, then Col. Waldrond, my self, and others, with no small pains, nor little Charge, contrived (as we thought) a Method, that might not only have laid the Duty on the Consumptioner, but also might have relieved you from the Complaints of those that does charge you with being great Debtors, and to have Enabled every Planter to make the best Advantage of their Plantations, by supplying them with Monies, at the

A Common

Co mon Interest of the Colonies, *by preventing numerous Sellers, necessitous and Ignorant Sales.*

And that this might run through the most strictest Examination before it should have been allowed of, We *proposed that his* Late Majesty *and* Privy-Council *might have the first view of it, that they might be satisfied it did not lessen his* Majesties Revenue, *and that* We *might have his* Majesties *leave to propose it to the* Assemblies *of every Individual* Collony, *and if they did approve of it, and Petition'd his* Majesty *for the Incorporating such Societies, that then we and our Friends might be Interested in it.*

But this meeting with Opposition, occasioned a Hearing before his Majesty *and the* Lords *of his* Privy-Council, *and after they were satisfied it did not lessen his* Majesties Revenue: *Our great debate with the Opposers was about his* Majesties *giving leave for the sending of it to the Collonies for them to Try and Examine it;* His Majesty *was pleased to declare, that he could not understand any reason could be given why they might not have a sight of it, for he thought* Barbado's *best knew what* Barbado's *wanted: I believe none will deny but that it met with a General Approbation of all the* Lords *of the* Council, *except my Lord* Chancellour, *of whom I was Informed by a Friend, (but at that time an Opposer of this design) that he was our Enemy, and Accordingly* We *found him.*

Soon after this hearing, the Government *began to be uneasy, and holding it not proper for a matter of this Nature, to be further proceeded on, under an* Unsetled Government, *I rather chose to be Silent, and to bear such Reflections that was made by those that were Totally Ignorant of the Method of our Undertaking, though Prejudiciall to my particular Interest, then to Expose it to view, before I saw the* Government *in a Temper to Consider of* Trade, *and the great benefit you are to this* Nation.

Therefore I have now Exposed it for your view, that you may be Judges whether it might have been, or may be Serviceable to you, and whether our request of sending it to you was unreasonable.

You will find by this Treatise *(as I humbly conceive) that our design would at least have raised the value of your Goods to the price it bore before the* Additional Duty *was laid, and it was allowed at that Hearing by the Opposers, that it would raise at least Twenty* per Cent. *Our Method was to have had all your* Goods *that came to* England

land *brought to one Body of Men, which we call'd a* Common Factory, *and they constantly to be chosen by you in your* Assemblies, *and they to have been Accountable to every* Consigner *for the Nett proceed of every parcell of Goods Sold, for which your Charge was not to exceed what you now pay . The other part of our design was to Erect a* Company, *separate from the* Common Factory, *which should have sufficient Funds in each* Collony, *to lend what Monies you had occasion of, you giving* Security *on* Lands *or* Goods, *and if they did not lend it, on demand, they were to forfeit to the* Borrower *considerable for every hundred Pound demanded, the* Lands *or* Goods *being valued by Sworn* Appraisers, *what was lent was to be continued during your Pleasure, you paying your Interest when due, and you had Power to pay it in, when you pleased, and they obliged to lend too at least one half value of* Land, *or* Goods, *and you not to have been confined to have borrowed it of them, but where else you pleased, so that this* Company *might have been* Serviceable, *but could not have been hurtfull, for they were bound to* Obey, *and had no Power to Command.*

To make it next to Impossibility, that the Government should ever be Imposed on, to permit any Laws *or* Designs *of any Persons whatsoever, let their pretences be ever so specious take effect, untill the* Collonies *by their* Assembly *were Consulted with : I have to the best of my knowledge given a True and Just Account of what Import, you are to this* Nation, *by Encreasing of* Navigation, *consuming the* Woollen-Manufactory, *of all sorts of* Apparell, Houshold-Goods, *&c. that are made in* England, *and that which was formerly* Forreign Commodities, *and cost us Considerable yearly, by your Industry, is become Native, the* Nation *freed from that Charge, and the* Consumptioner *saves at least one half of his Expence for the like quantity ; Besides the great Advantage this* Nation *receives by your* Goods *Exported, being over and above our Consumption ; And Lastly, all the Riches you get in the* Indies *by your great Care, Labour, and Industry, is brought to* England, *and here it Centers.*

If you will be pleased to rectify my Errours, that I through Ignorance may have Committed, that our Legislators may be more fully satisfy'd, that you are and ever must be English-Men, *and that you are much more beneficially Employed there, for the Benefit of this* Nation, *than any the like Number in* England, *that every hardship that is put upon you, that makes your* Goods *dearer in* Forreign Markets, *or lessens the*

Consumption

Confumption *in* England, *is a leſſening to the Trade of* England, *and conſequently prejudicial to every Subject in* England: *and if this ſmall Treatiſe, meets with your kind Acceptance, I ſhall think my ſelf very happy, and ſhall always be ready to demonſtrate, that I am your Wellwiſher, and* Gentlemen,

    Your Moſt Humble and

     Faithfull Servant.

      Dalby Thomas.

CAP. I.

CAP. I.

Here is nothing more frequent amongſt the Generality of Mankind than is the drawing wrong Conclusions from right Premiſes, whereby the moſt concife and trueſt Maxims and ſayings that wife Men upon ſolid thinking have contriv'd to guide us like Landmarks in the ſearch of Truth, are perverted by wrong Applications to drown our Underſtandings in the Gulph of Errour.

Thus becauſe Truth it ſelf is not truer, than that People are the Wealth of a Nation, thoſe who have not time, experience, and skill, to examine the Fond of that undeniable verity, tho' in other things Men of Excellent Underſtandings are apt to inferr, that all who ſet foot out of the Kingdom are in ſome degree a diminution of its Wealth, and thence take for granted that the *American* Coilonies occaſion the decay both of the People and Riches of the Nation, when upon a thorough Examination nothing can appear more Erroneous, as I doubt not to make plain to every man, tho' my principal deſign is to convince the Nobility and Gentry of the Kingdom who being the Contrivers of our Statutes and moſt concern'd for the Preſervation of its Grandeur ought rightly to be Inform'd, for fear our Laws in time take a contrary Byaſs to our Trade and Navigation, which are undeniably our Glory and Strength, as well as the only Fountain of our Riches.

To make this point clear it is neceſſary to Conſider and Examine Four things,
1. What is Real Wealth:
2. What is Imaginary Wealth:
3. How theſe are acquir'd:
4. How they may be loſt.

To diſtinguiſh rightly in theſe points we muſt conſider Money as the leaſt part of the Wealth of any Nation, and think of it only as a Scale to weigh one thing againſt another, Or as Counters to reckon Riches by, or as a pawn of Intrinſique value to depoſite in lieu of any neceſſary whatſoever.

True, Solid, and real Wealth therefore in reſpect to the Nation is the Land, and what is upon or under its ſurface, as uſefull Buildings, Trees, Quarries, Mines, &c.

Thus by a good Computation made by Sir *William Petty*, which we will take for granted till there appears a better, We may reckon the preſent Rent of Land and Houſes to be 10000000*l.* *per Annum*, which at 20 years purchaſe amounts to 200000000*l.*

The People of this Nation conſume Annually in neceſſary Meat, Drink and Cloaths, computed from their Numbers, manner of Living, and uſuall price Current of things about 50000000*l.* Annually, which is about 6*l.* 10*s.* a Head.

The Imaginary Wealth therefore of the Nation which conſiſts in Labour, Trade, and Negotiation, is four times as much as the Reall, And Preſerved in its natural Channels, is to be reduced to the ſame Value in Purchaſe as Land ; whereby we may allow, that the Intrinſick worth of the People and Kingdom as they now ſtand together, is 1000000000*l*

The Money in Species of the Nation, tho' the Scale by which the whole is valued and weighed, amounts not to 6000000*l.*

Now ſuch as do account the Lands and Buildings of the Nation more valuable, becauſe Real, then the Negotiation, becauſe Accidentall and Imaginary, will find themſelves miſtaken, ſince Lands and Houſes without People are of no value at all, and to a Naked, and uninduſtrious Nation very little more, ſo that Labour, Invention, Trade, and Negotiation, are the only Cauſes of as well as Supports to that we call Riches.

This is ſo ſelf-Evident that it will be ſuperfluous to Illuſtrate it by many examples or Compariſons between Civil and Barbarous Countrys.

Therefore we muſt Conſider, that when it is ſaid, People are the Wealth of a Nation, It is only meant, Laborious and Induſtrious People, and not ſuch as are wholly unemploy'd, as Gentry, Clergy, Lawyers, Servingmen, and Beggars, &c. Or which is worſe, Employ'd only in diſturbing the Induſtrious and Laborious, as Pettifoggers, Informers, Catchpoles and Theeves ; And tho' the firſt ſorts may be be neceſſary, as harmleſs Spurs to Conſumption, Learning or Vertue, or as objects of the good will, mutuall Love, Pitty and Compaſſion of Humane Nature, as well as Increaſers of the Numbers by Children, yet the fewer ſuch the better, whereas the laſt ſhould by all Imaginary ways be diſcouraged, tam'd or deſtroy'd as the worſt of Vermine in a well-Govern'd Common-wealth.

We muſt likewiſe conſider, that the value of every thing uſefull to the neceſſities, Luxuries, or Vanities of Life, is meaſured by the Induſtry and Labour either of Body or Mind, which is neceſſary to their Acquirement, whereby things of little or no price in one Country, by the time ſpent, Labour and hazard of thoſe which carry them to Another become dear.

From all which it is plain that only Induſtrious and Laborious People are the Riches of any Nation, And it will as naturally follow, that theſe Laborious or Induſtrious which Employ their Tallents to moſt Advantage, are of moſt value to ſuch Nation.

And tho' a Man whoſe skill amounts to no more than to Earn 3d. a Day by his continuall Labour, can no ways add to the Wealth of a Kingdom like Ours, becauſe it will not ſupply his neceſſary Conſumption, yet ſuch a Man is a leſs burthen to it than one totally Idle, and may Increaſe the number by Children.

So again, One that conſtantly by his Labour can Earn 6d. a Day only, and Conſumes juſt ſo much, as he is not Advantageous to the Nations Wealth, ſo he is no Burthen neither, and occaſions its Increaſe.

But that Man who by Induſtry and Labour not only maintains himſelf and Family, but makes himſelf Rich, is to the proportion of his Wealth juſt ſo much Addition to the Intrinſique value of the Kingdom.

I have the more Enlarged upon this head, that I might lead the mind of the Reader by a naturall Chain of Conſequences rightly to underſtand the true Original and Everlaſting ſupport of Wealth, which is nothing elſe but Labour.

As for ſuch Perſons who by the faculties of the mind only acquire Riches to themſelves, as Soldiers, Lawyers, Divines, Bankers, Retailers, Victuallers, &c. They tho' neceſſary Callings, are no Increaſers of the Nations Wealth, nor is the Kingdom more rich by the Fluctuating and Circulation of Money among ſuch than one of them would be by putting his Money out of one Cheſt into another, or ſhifting it from one pocket to another.

But where Soldiery becomes the Trade of a People, as among the

Switzers and *Scots* it is, who serve abroad for money, and brings it home to purchase Lands there, it is of equall benefit to any other Labour, by Increasing the Rates and value of the reall Wealth of those Countries, which as amongst all other Civill Nations is Land and Houses.

I doubt not but the Reader by this time will perceive, that in what way soever a Man Employs his Labour and Industry either at home or abroad, so that at last he Increases the value of the Real Wealth of the Nation, he is in the proportion of such Increase a benefit thereunto.

And on the Contrary, he that Labours not at all, or so much as not to Increase the Intrinsick value of his Countrey, is just good for Nothing.

To leave this Truth plain beyond dispute, I beg the doubter but to Consider, that if all the Laborious People of the Kingdom left working, and were to live upon the naturall produce of it, to be distributed to them in equall proportions by way of Charity, as Parish-poor and Beggars are now supported, how long it would be before the Nation became necessitous, Naked and Starving, and Consequently the Land and Houses worth nothing.

A short Reflexion would make him sensible that a very few years of Idleness would Compleat the matter, whence he can no longer doubt, but that Labour and Industry rightly apply'd, is the Sole cause of the Wealth of a Nation, that Money is only the Scales or Touchstone to weigh or value things by: And that Land it self would yield no Rent but as Labour Employ'd for the support of Luxuries, as well as necessities, did find a due Incouragement and Increase.

In short it is plain hereby,

1. That Reall Wealth is Land and Houses;
2. That Imaginary Wealth is the Laborious People.
3. That the Reall and Imaginary Wealth both Increase only, as Industry is rightly apply'd by great Numbers of Laborious People: And not by Increase of People only.
4. And the Increase of People willfully or Accidentally Idle, is so far from being National Riches, that it is the surest and speediest way to Inevitable Poverty, Famine and Nakedness, and must decay the value as well of the Reall as Imaginary Wealth of the Nation, proportionably to the decay of Industry.

Thus Civil Wars, Disorders, and Changes in the Government of Nations, by the many which become Soldiers, and others that cease labouring in their Trades and Industry, for want of security, insensibly

sibly impoverish Countries, much more than those slain in such Changes do; By reason that those that dye, as they add nothing, do consume nothing in the Common-wealth; whereas the Idle Living, add nothing, and consume much to its Destruction.

I shall say no more therefore on this Subject, but hasten to the Consideration of which hands are best Employ'd to the Advantage of the Wealth of this Kingdom, as our Trade and Negociation now stand.

First then, the Premisses consider'd we may lay down as an undeniable verity, That those Men who add most by their Labour to the Increase of the Intrinsick Wealth of the Nation, either Reall or Imaginary, and Consume least, are best Employ'd.

Again, on the Contrary, those that Consume most and add least, are worst Imploy'd.

Now it will be Impossible in the short method I design, to Enumerate and clearly distinguish between every Sort of Employment, wherefore I shall content my self only to hint at some few ways wherein men seem to do little, and yet are well employ'd, And others wherein they are very busy and Laborious to little or no purpose.

To begin then as nature did in the Cultivators of Land and Conductors of Cattle.

The Husbandmans Life not only seems but is extreamly Carefull, Laborious and Painfull: The Grasier and Shepheards on the Contrary, both seems and is a very Carelefs quiet and easy way of spending time.

Yet tho' the first sort are usually paid most wages, and consequently can afford and do consume most upon themselves, the last notwithstanding are of much more value to the Comonwealth.

For 200. Sheep or 20. Cows require but 40. Acres of good Land, and one mans easy Care for a years pasture, the profit of which by the Increase of Lambs, Calves, Wooll, Butter, Cheese, &c. And the Meliorating the Wooll by Manufacture, is of four times at least more advantage to the Comonwealth, then the same number of Acres imploy'd in Tillage, which requires the constant Drudgery of two men and four horses at least; besides that the greatest part of what is produced by Tillage is consumed in the Nation: whereas Manufactured Wooll from Sheep, Tallow, Leather, Shoos, Butter, Cheese, Salt, Beef, and many other things, arising from pasture, are Staple Comodities for Transportation, which fetch us back Silver, Gold, and foreign goods, usefull to the Ornament and Pleasure, if not necessities of Life: I must affirm, the Comodity which is Transported is the only true increase of Nationall Strength and Wealth, and that fort of Reformers who would have nothing made, us'd, or confumed, but what Nature abfolutely requires, are but fhort-fighted and narrow thinkers as well in Politicks as Religion : And tho' they may adorn their opinions and Arguments with the names of *Lycurgus*, *Cato*, and other Sour-Reafoners, yet all their Difcourfes tend to no more but to reduce Mankind back to be Sheep-skin-Wearers, Acorn-Eaters, and waterDrinkers: again, The bountifull God of nature, fupplying every Country of the World with what is fully fufficie, t to fuftain Life.

Therefore to fay, as many are apt to do, that *England* can live of it felf without the affiftance of any Forreign Nation, is to give it not the leaft Commendation beyond any other Country : but to fay, and that truly, that *England* by the Induftry of its Inhabitants imploy'd in Shipping, Plantations, Mines, Manufactures, Paftures and Tillage, doth not only abound in all forts of Commodities, as Native Meat, Drink, Cloaths, Houfes and Coaches, fit for the neceffities, Eafe, and Ornaments of Life, but can outvy moft Nations of the World for the vaft plenty in varieties of Wines, Spices, Drugs, Fruits, Silks, Pictures, Mufick, Silver, Gold, Precious Stones, and all other the fupports of Grandeur and Delight, That is to fpeak it, a truly Civiliz'd and Glorious Nation indeed.

And tho' fome Men thro' falfe and envious Opticks look upon thefe things as baits to Vice, and occafions of Effeminency, if they would but impartially examine the truth of matters, they would difcern them to be the true Spurs to Virtue, Valour and the Elevation of the mind, as well as the juft rewards of Induftry. For,

It is certain, upon a right Scrutiny, a man fhall finde more profanenefs, difhonefty, Drunkennefs and Debauchery, practifed in nafty Rags, bare-walls and Alehoufes, than in rich Habits, Pallaces, or Taverns ; and as Plenty, Splendour, and Grandure, can have no other Fountain but Wifdom, Induftry and good conduct ; fo Shabbinefs, Indigence and Contempt, rarely fpring from any thing but Folly, Idlenefs and Vice : And where it happens otherways. by unexpected Frauds, fhipwracks, Fires, Inundations or maymes, the fhame of fuffering it becomes the Nations reproach, fince the rarity of thefe Accidents would make the Burden which Crufhes a particular Scarce felt when laid by a right method on the whole Comonwealth, as I fhall endeavour to make appear hereafter.

But before I return again to the confideration which part of the people are beft employ'd for the publick good, I muft from what is premifed, mised, Conclude, that as all who are not mischeivously employ'd or totally Idle, are of some Benefit to the Comonwealth, and should find due encouragement, so those ought to be most protected and least discouraged by the Laws who are most usefully busy for the Increasing the Value of the Real and Imaginary Wealth of the Nation: Thus as I said before, the Shepheard and Grazier is to be preferr'd before the Plowman and Thrasher.

So the Miner is to be preferr'd to the Shepheard and Grazier, because all he produces for Transportation, is clear Gains to the publick, whereas but part of the others doth so: The Marriner is to be prefer'd to the Miner, and the like to such who Contribute most to forreign Trade, but in *England* the Merchant-Adventurer is to be encouraged and prefer'd before the Marriner, or any other Artist, Trade or Calling whatsoever: For tho' his labour seems a Recreation rather than a Toil, and consists chiefly in a regular Methodizing of a punctuall Rotation of Credit, and change of Commodities from one place to another; Yet considering that the whole produce of Nature and Art would be but dead matter without a proper motion to Convey it to its true end which is Consumption: All other Callings receive their Vigour, Life, Strength and Increase from the Merchant, Commodities rising in Esteem or Value as they are rightly distributed from place to place, and loosing their very nature as well as worth, when by overstocking the Market they become Contemptible, or perish for want of use or consumption: Wherefore our Laws should be so contriv'd as never in the least to discourage or check any Conception or Endeavour of the Venturing Merchant, to whose Extravagant and hazardous, as well as prudent and cautious undertaking, this Nation chiefly Ows all its Wealth and Glory: And it is a mighty pitty that all Laws for Custome and Dutyes, as well as for regulating Navigation, Erecting Companies, Judging Maritine Controversies, granting Letters of Mart and Repriseall, and for Encouraging Manufactures and Societies of Handicrafts, should not first be debated, prepar'd and begun in a great Councell of Trade, to consist of members Elected and Deputed by every Plantation, Marritime, City, Company, Constitution and Trade, which would desire to send Members to it: And from thence after a free and full examination be represented to both Houses of Parliament for their Approbation or Dislike.

For Trade is of that Nature, that it requires frequent Pruning, Lopping, and Restraining, as well as Cultivating and Cherishing, and thrives much better under proper and rightly apply'd Restrains, Duties.

ties, Taxes and Excises, than in a general loosenefs, which being so, is it possible that a positive Tonnage and Poundage like ours should hit all Accidents, attend the Changes and Mutations it receives, both at Home by the Plenty and Scarcity of our Native Commodities, or Abroad by the like Ebbs and Floods as well as the Laws in Forreign Nations made or chang'd concerning it.

Or how indeed can the Divines, Lawyers, Nobility, and great Gentry of the Kingdom be Nice Judges, and right distinguishers between the Clashing and Tangling Interests of so great a Mistery as Universal Trade, when few or none of them have ever had the least occasion to Inspect or Experiment any part of it.

The defect therefore of a free and able Council of Trade in this Nation, tho' it cannot destroy, yet wonderfully retards and hinders the Natural and Genuine Increase of Navigation and Merchandise, and consequently of Rents.

But for want of that, I will presume to go on in Explaining the Right and Wrong Application of Mens Industry, as they respect in generall the Wealth and Grandeur of the Nation, or in particular the Interest of Our *American* Collonies, in many of which I doubt not to demonstrate. One Labouring Man is of more Advantage to *England*, tho' out of it, than any thirty the like kind can be within it.

To Explain which, I will take a short view of our Sugar-Plantations, and the nature of that Trade, to whose particular advantage and Interest after the Kingdoms, I principally sacrifice my present pains.

I therefore with all Submissiveness imaginable, desire Our Legislators to Consider,

1. That the greatest Consumption of Sugar is made by themselves, and the rest of the Rich and Opulent People of the Nation, tho' usefull to all degrees of Men.

2. That the quantity of yearly produced within those Sugar Collonies, is not less then 45000 Tons English Tonnage, each comprehending 20*l*. to the Ton.

3. That about the Moiety of that is Consumed in *England*.

4. That the Medium of the Value of consumed Sugar at the present price Currant is 4*d*. a pound.

5. That the quantity Consumed in the Nation at that price amounts to 800000*l*. Sterling, and upwards.

6. That the other Moiety sent to Forreign Markets after it has Employ'd Seamen, and Earn'd Freight, is sold for as much, and consequently brings back to the Nation in Money or usefull Goods Annually 800000*l*.

800000*l*, which is more than any one other Commodity doth.

7. Consider too, that before Sugars were produced in our own Collonies, it bore three times the Price it doth now, so that by the same Consumption, at the same price, except we made it our selves, we should be forced to give in Money, or Moneys worth, as Native Commodities and Labour 2400000*l*. for the Sugar we spend, or be without it to such a degree of disadvantage of well Living, as that Retrenchment would amount to; We must Consider too, that the Spirits arising from *Mellasses* which is sent from the Sugar Collonies to the other Collonies, and to *England*, which if all were sold in *England* and turn'd into Spirits, it would Amount annually to above 500000*l*. at half the price the like quantity of *Brandy* from *France* would cost, and will yearly Increase as *Brandies* are discouraged, and by most are held wholsomer for the Body, which is observed by the long living of those in the Collonies that are great Drinkers of Rum, which is the Spirits we make of *Mellasses*, and the short living of those that are great Drinkers of *Brandy* in those parts.

The *Indico* coming thence amounts to 50000*l*. per *Ann*.

The *Logwood* for which we formerly paid the *Spaniards* 100*l*. per *Ton*, now comes under 15*l*. and amounts to 1000 Ton Annually.

The *Cotton* for which we paid formerly above 12*d*. per *pound*, now comes at 5*d* ½. per *pound*. and amounts to 1000 Ton per *Annum*, besides the Hands it Employs in Manufacturing it.

The *Ginger* amounts to 4000 Ton per *annum*, and is not the Sixth part in price of what the Nation paid formerly for that Commodity, or for *Pepper* instead of it.

Not to speak of the many *Druggs*, *Woods*, *Cocoa*, *Piemento*, and *Spices*, besides *Raw-Hides* &c. which comes from those parts, nor of the great quantity of the Gold, and Silver we have of the *Spaniards* for *Negroes*, and English Manufactory carryed by our sloops from our Collonies to them.

So that it is demonstration, the Nation saves and gains by the People Employ'd in those Collonies 4000000*l*. Sterling per *An*.

Now if it be Consider'd that in all those *Sugar Collonies* there is not 600000 white Men Women and Children, it necessarily must follow, that one with another above what they consume each of them Earns for the Publick above 6*l*. per *ann*.

(10)

Whereas if the Rent be 10000000,
And the Confumption 50000000,
Then by reducing Labour and Confumption to a proper Ballance with the produce of Rents, and suppofing the Imaginary Wealth of the whole Kingdom to Increafe in time of Peace, the Tenth part Annually that will be but four Millions, which does not Amount to Twelve Shillings a Head clear Increafe of Wealth, One with another, above neceffary and conftant Expences, from which it follows beyond Controverfy, that hands Employ'd in the Sugar-Plantations are one with another of 130 times the value to the Common-wealth than thofe which ftay at home.

To this I eafily forefee will be readily Objected, for want of Confideration, that thofe there confume nothing of Native Commodities, which if they did as thefe do which ftay at home, their Confumption would amount to 390000*l.* Annually at *6l.* 10*s.* 0*d.* per Head. as afore-faid, and would confequently Increafe the Rents at leaft a Fourth of that.

But to this I muft reminde the Reader that I have demonftrated, that whatever is Confum'd by Idle Men, can never Increafe either the Reall or Imaginary Wealth of the Nation, and that nothing but the Overplus or Confumption can be reckon'd Additional Wealth, which according to our Reafonable Computation cannot be above 2*s.* a head, one with another, So that if we would grant that thofe in the Collonies did Confume nothing of our home produce, the lofs by want of them here could amount only to 1200000*s.* Annually, which is 60000*l.*

But on the contrary, this is fo far from being true, that one with another each White Man, Woman, and Child, refiding in the Sugar-Plantations, occafions the Confumption of more of our Native Commodities, and Manufactures then ten at home do.

This cannot be doubted by thofe that will Confider the great quantity of Beef, Pork, Salt, Fifh, Butter, Cheefe, Corn and Flower, as well as Beer, Englifh-Mum, Syder and Coals, conftantly fent thither, of which Commodities for the ufe of themfelves or Blacks, they have little or none of their own produce: Confider too, that all their Powder, Cannon, Swords, Guns, Pikes, and other Weapons, their Cloaths, Shoes, Stockings, Sadles, Bridles, Coaches, Beds, Chairs, Stools, Pictures, Clocks, and Watches, their Pewter,
Brafs,

Brafs, Copper and Iron Veffels and Inftruments, their Sail-Cloath, and Cordage, of which in their Building, Shipping, Mills, Boyling and Diftilling-Houfes, Field-Labour and Domeftick ufes, they Confume infinite quantities, all which are made in and fent from *England*: Not to fpeak of the great number of Drudging and Saddle Horfes they take off, as well as of that fort of People who would in their Youth be confumed in Idlenefs, or worfe at home, but there become ufefull to Increafe the Nations, Numbers, and Wealth both.

Befides, it muft be remembred, that there is in thofe Collonies at leaft 5 Blacks for one White, fo that allowing the Whites to be 60000, the Blacks muft be 300000, all whofe Cloaths and European Provifions coming from *England*, Increafes the Confumption of our Native Commodities and Manufactures in a large Proportion. But the Axes, Hoes, Saws, Rollers, Shovells, Knives, Nails, and other Iron Inftruments and Tools as well as the Boylers, Stills, and other ufefull Veffells of Copper, Lead and Pewter, which are wafted, Confumed and Deftroy'd by the Induftry and profitable Labour of that mighty Number of Slaves, are not eafily to be Computed, but muft plainly and beyond all Contradiction be of great Advantage to the Nation as well as to thofe Induftrious People Employ'd at home in making them.

If thefe things with the vaft quantity of Shipping that thofe Collonies Employ, be in the leaft reflected on, it will open the Eyes of the moft unexperienced Perfon in the Trade, to difcern the mighty advantage the Nation receives from thofe People which go to thofe Collonies, and the great Obligation there lyes upon our Legiflators to Study their due Improvement, fafety and Increafe.

For befides all the benefits demonftrably coming to the Nation as aforefaid, They are in fome kind Maritime Armies, ever ready not only to Defend themfelves but to punifh the Exorbitances, Incroachments, Piracies, and Depradations of any Infulting Neighbouring Nation; Nor is it to be imagin'd in what Awe thofe Collonies rightly managed might keep our *French*, *Spanifh*, *Dutch*, *Danifh*, *Brandenburgh* and *Hamburgh* Rivalls, for Wealth and Maritime Power from Entring into any Treaties, Alliances or Undertakings, to our Difadvantage.

What has been faid fhall ferve for an Introduction in Generall to the more particular parts of the Nations Interest in the *American* Trade, and the due Encouragement it ought to receive from the Laws which may naturally make us the most Rich and Florishing part, as well as the undoubted Arbitrators of *Europe*, if not of all the Maritime Nations of the World. And in the next place, I will show what Discouragements those Collonies lye under at present.

C A P.

CAP. II.

The better to Explain this to every Capacity, it will be neceſſary to make a ſhort Hiſtory of *Sugar*, that the Invention, Planting, and divers uſes of it being known, the Reader may thereby make a more perfect Judgement of the Nationall Intereſt therein.

To which purpoſe it is firſt to be Conſider'd, that the *Europeans* 500 years ſince, were perfect Strangers to the uſe of it, and ſcarcely knew its name; but the *Venetians* about that time being the great Traders in *Eaſt-India* Spices, Gums, and Drugs, did amongſt other rarities introduce *Sugar*, which the Phyſitians ſoon found to anſwer all the ends of Honey, without many of its ill effects; So that it quickly became a Commodity in mighty eſteem, and though the price then was ten times more then now, yet it prevailed ſo faſt, and the Conſumption of it became ſo great, that an ill way of making, planting, and Curing of it, was about 300 years ſince found out and practiſed in *Greece*, and ſome other neighbour Nations, where the heat of the Sun could in any degree ripen the Cane.

But no Nation made ſo conſiderable a progreſs therein as the *Portugalls*, who having with ſome Succeſs, Improv'd the Art of Planting it in their *Affrican* Collonies and Iſlands, did at laſt make it their main Buſineſs in *Braſile*, becoming thereby the only Nation that ſet the price upon it to all the parts of the World, untill the *Hollanders* grew their Rivalls for Power and profit in that part of *America*.

But about 50 years ſince, during the war between thoſe two Nations in *Braſile*, a *Hollander* happen'd to arrive from thence upon our Iſland of *Barbados*, where though there were good *Sugar-Canes*, The Engliſh knew no other uſe of them than to make refreſhing Drink for that hot Climate, intending by planting Tobacco there,

to

to have equall'd those of the *Verina's*, on which, Ginger, Cotten and Indico they meant to rely ; But this *Hollander* understanding Sugar, was by one Mr. *Drax*, and some other Inhabitants there drawn into to make Discovery of the Art he had to make it ; since which time by the many ingenious men the last Civill war necessitated to seek their fortunes in that new world, there has been found out so many severall sorts of Mills, Coppers, Boylers, Stoves, Pots, and other Tools and Engins, for Planting and pressing the Canes, Boyling-up, Separating, Cleansing, and Purifying the Juice and Sugar, as well as for drawing Spirits of admirable use from the Mellasses, that we at present exceed all the Nations in the world in the true Improvement of that Noble Juice of the Cane, which next to that of the Vine, exceeds all the Liquors in the World. And as our Nation has been ever famous for Meliorating Inventions of all kinds, so in this we have gone so far, that notwithstanding the many Discouragements, those Planters do at present and have heretofore lain under, yet they apparently set the Price of it in all *Europe*, to the Kingdoms Pleasure, Glory, and Grandure; which are all more advanc'd by that, than by any other Commodity we deal in or produce, Wooll not excepted ; as I doubt not but to Demonstrate beyond all Dispute before I end these Papers : which that I may the better do as well as show clearly the mighty Interest the nation has in preserving our *West-India* Collonies, I will give the Reader a clear and short Account of a Sugar, a Cotton, a Ginger, and Indico Plantation, as they are now managed in *Barbados*; and then set down a short Scheme of the raising and producing Tobacco, which though in it self perhaps not absolutely, if at all necessary to well Living, yet having prevail'd so far upon the Vitiated Humours of men, as we see it has, is of great concern to us, as well for bringing in Wealth as Employing multitudes of men in Manufacture and Navigation, which no man can Dispute but to be a true Nationall Interest.

   100 Acres of Land Employ'd in a Sugar-Plantation will require 50 Black Slaves and 7 white Servants to Manage it.

   There must be 6 Horses and 8 Oxen for two Teams.

   There must be an Overseer at 20*l* per *annum*, a Doctor and Farrier at 20*l. per annum*, and a Carter at 12*l. per annum*.

   20 of the 100 Acres must be set apart for Pasture, provisions, and

and a Nurſery for Canes to Plant with.

 40 of the remaining Acres return a Crop one year, and 40 the next, and ſo allternatively, being Conſtantly now to be replanted after every Cutting, whereas when the ground was firſt broke up, the ſame Canes would yield two three or more Cuttings before they were replanted, to the wonderfull eaſe and advantage of the firſt Planters.

 There muſt be a Windmill which turns great Iron Rollers, between which the Cane is preſs'd.

 There muſt be a Boiling-houſe, and in it Boylers Coolers, Receivers, and Ciſterns, to which belong Ladles, Scummers, and Lamps, &c.

 A Sill-houſe with Ciſterns, Stills, Worms, worm-Tubs, &c.

 A Curing-houſe, with Earthen Sugar-pots, Drips and Ciſterns for Mellaſſes.

 A Drying-houſe with neceſſaries.

 A Houſe for the neceſſary Fewell Employ'd in Boyling and Stilling.

 A Houſe for Knocking out, Packing, and Storing of Sugar.

 A Dwelling-houſe, with Houſes for Servants and Negroes.

 A Houſe for Cattle, beſides Carts, Hooks, Hoes, and other Planting-Utenſills, the firſt coſt whereof will with utmoſt Husbandry amount to 5625*l*. the Wear and Tear whereof will not be leſs annually than 60*l*.

 A Plantation of 100 Acres well ſtockt and provided as aforeſaid, and manag'd to its full height, without thoſe accidentall Caſualties which often, may probably produce annually 80 hogſheads of Sugar of 1000 pound weight each hogſhead, that is 2000 pound weight of Muſcovado Sugar from each Acre, and of Mellaſſes 20 hogſheads of 700 pound weight each hogſhead.

 This Sugar in the Iſland may be valued at 10*s. per* hundred, as it may be at home at 20*s*. that being as the price has gone ſince the additionall Duty was laid, the *Medium* of what Muſcovado Sugars have yielded; all which with the prime Coſt as well as the Mellaſſes Rum, &c. ſhall be brought to a rationall and equall Ballance, after a little more has been ſaid of the manner of Planting, making and Refining Sugars.

 The firſt thing is done to that ground deſign'd for planting, is
with

with Hoes by the labour of Negro's to open and loosen the Surface of the Earth to Prepare in for the Plants.

There is commonly two Seasons, Rainy and Dry, the Rainy begins in *May* or *June*, and ends in *December* or *January*, all which is spent in Hoeing, Dunging and Planting the Canes.

The Dry Season is spent in Cutting the Canes, Grinding them at the Mills, Boyling up the Liquor, and making thereof Muscovado Sugar; All which must of necessity go hand in hand together, for the Cane must be prest as it is Cut, or the Juice drys in it; The Juice must be boyled up to it's proper Consistency for grayning as soon as prest, or it will Sour and perish; The grayn must be Separated speedily, whilst hot, from the Mollasses, or they will Cling together, ferment and grow Sour in time again, or be at best but fit for the Still.

But as for Refining and Stilling, that any Season is fit for.

Thus it is to be observ'd, that the Blacks are always Employ'd either in Hoeing, Dunging, and Planting in the wet, or in Cutting, Carrying, Grinding, Boyling, &c. In the Dry Seasons.

There are divers ways of producing new Plants, as by cutting the Root of an Old Plant, by laying a Cane in the Ground, By Planting the Top of a Cane cut off, or by taking a shoot from a Knot of a Cane, many of which will have 5 or 6 that put in the ground will grow; But the generall way is from those have been set in the Nurseries, for from one Root there will proceed divers shoots, all fit for Planting as 9 or 10, and sometimes 20.

The ground being prepar'd, Holes are made therein, and in every Hole Dung put, and then a Plant, which in 18 Months or thereabouts, becomes fit for Cutting, so that half a year being spent in graduall planting, 40 Acres, 6 or 7 Acres a month will be ready Successively to be Cut in the proper Season, so that 80. Acres is a just Employment for the continuall Labour 50 Blacks and 7 Whites in the field, and for 3 others for overseeing, Carting and Curing the Plantations.

When the Canes are prest by passing through the Rollers of a Windmill, there runs from thence a great quantity of pleasant Juice, which being put into Boylers by the heat of the fire, having Evaporated the Flegm or Watry matter to such a time as it becomes of a proper Consistency, then they throw it into a mixture

consisting

consisting of some materiall fit to cleanse it and prepare it for graining; all the time it is Boyling with large Copper Scummers they take off the Scum which constantly rises in great quantities, untill it be fit to Empty into Coolers, from whence it is again sifted into Earthen Pots with holes in their bottoms, and Pots they call Drips under them, for receiving the Moisture call'd Mellasses, which in about a months time will be separated from that which is then called Muscovado Sugar, being of a pale Yellow Collour; this is then knockt out of the pots, and put into Caskes for Transportation.

This sort of Mellasses is either Boyl'd up again to extract from it a sort of a Duskish pale grey Sugar call'd Panneels, or sent in Cask for *England* as the Sugar is.

The Scum that arises with all the washings of the Boylers, Coolers, Pots, and other Instruments Employ'd in that Business, is preserv'd in great Cisterns where it will ferment and becomes fit for stilling.

The Spirits proceeding from Mellasses and this effect of good Husbandry is called Rum, being a Noble Intoxicating Liquor, which the Negroes as well as English Servants but too much delight in, and the Planters themselves prefer some sorts of it to any Brandy either for Punch or other uses where Spirits are needed.

And with truth this may be said of the Sugar Cane, that it produces nothing but what is of great use to well living; The Vertues of Mellasses formerly sold only in Apothecary's Shops by the name of Treacle being now so well known both to the Distiller and Brewer, that a great part of their Estates are owing to it: Nor can it be imagin'd how many new ways are found dayly for Venting and Consuming usefully the various products of a Sugar-Plantation: The severall Shapes it appears in at Christenings, Banquets, and Rich mens Tables, being but the least of its good qualities, tho' of great Delight as well as Ornament, and should the art of making it be so discouraged as to take its next flight to the *Dutch* or *French*, as it did from *Portugall* to Us, The loss would prove of the like Consequence, which is no less than the Decay of the greatest part of their Shipping, and the fall of half their Revenues: they being forc'd to abate 10 *per Cent*. Duty lately, to get some to be Exported, and that with little or no Success.

D   And

And yet inevitably this mifchief will happen if great Care be not taken to preferve thofe Collonies.

But to return to the further Hiftory of a Plantation, and making and Improving Sugars, it is to be remembred, that to compleat a Sugar-work of an hundred Acres, the neceffary Charges as aforefaid will be ———— In 50 Blacks   1250*l*.
      7 white Servants befides three Artifts
       which are pay'd wages———   150*l*.
         5 Horfes———   125*l*.
         8 Bullocks———   100*l*.
    Land, Houfes, Mills, Veffells, *&c.*
    All other Tools and Implements 4000*l*.
                       In all 5625*l*.

Which Plantation Ordinarily may produce as aforefaid anually in Mufcovado Sugars Eighty Hogfheads: In Mellaffes twenty eight Hogfheads, both which in the *Weft-Indies* at the *Medium* of the price now currant, will yield five hundred and forty pound. So that 10 white Servants Employ'd as aforefaid Earn five hundred and forty pound, which is fifty four pound a head.

The *Englifh* Cloaths and provifions fuch 10 whites and 50 Blacks confume is one with another forty fhillings a head, and amounts to an hundred and twenty pound.

The Wear and Tear of the Tools and neceffary Supplys of a Plantation from *England* is as leaft fixty pound.

In all an hundred and eighty pound.

So that confidering the 10 white people in a Plantation are the Sole caufe of that Confumption it is eighteen pound each, which as I faid before is a far greater Confumption on the native Commodities and Manufactures of the Nation than Labourers at home make, and it ought to be confider'd too, that in this Ballance I have not Computed the firft coft of the Materials that fet all thefe ufefull Labourers at work, nor the profit has arifen to Navigation, and the Merchant Adventurer in fending thither near a Million of Slaves, whofe firft coft to the Planter has been Eight Millions of Pounds at leaft, and took off of our Manufacture to buy them in *Guinnea* about Forty Shillings *per head*, which amounts to Two Millions; Not to fpeak in this place neither of the Rich Cloaths, Houfhold Stuff, and other neceffaries, the Mafters of thefe Numerous

(19)

Servants confume upon themfelves, which without an Exact Account or Scrutiny into every particular, muft fatisfy the moft prejudic'd Perfon that the People there both for Addition of Wealth and Confumption of Commodities are better Employ'd than thofe which remain at Home.

But to add to a Plantation as aforefaid the advantage arifing by Refining Sugar, there muft be laid out in a Refining-Houfe, Coppers, and all other neceffary Materials, at leaft Three hundred Pound. There muft be Ten Blacks, and no Whites if the Boylers can Refine which is eafy to Learn.

The manner thus they take their *Mufcovado* Sugars, and put it into Refining Coppers mixt with Lime-Water, where as it Boyls over a gentle Fire, much Scum will arife, which is taken off conftantly till it become to a fufficient Confiftency for mixing it with the whites of Eggs well beaten up, which being done in order to Clarify it 'tis then boyl'd to a proper height for Refined Sugar, and turn'd off into Coolers, and thence put into fuch Pots with their Dripps as was faid of *Mufcovado*'s: When thefe Pots have ftood Dripping Eight or Ten Days, then Clay properly temper'd is put upon the Pots, which is renew'd as occafion requires, this forces down all the Melaffes, fo that in Seven or Eight Weeks thefe Sugar's fo Improv'd will be fit for Casking.

The Melaffes thus Iffuing from Refined Sugar is Boyled up again, and Operated as before, produces a Sugar called Baftardwhites, the laft Melaffes being only fit for the Still.

Note that little or Nothing of the quantity is wafted in the Refining, but remains in Sugar Melaffes or Liquor, from which Spirit is produced.

But let be obferved too, that by the Additional Stock of Ten Blacks which coft two hundred pound; Houfe and neceffaries three hundred pound; neceffary Provifion for the Ten Blacks Twenty pound Wear and Tear Thirty pound; Intereft for the firft Coft at Ten pound *per Cent.* Fifty pound: In all a hundred pound *per Ann.* A Plantation is near doubled. So that is is plainly the Intereft of the Nation that all Sugars fhould be fully Meliorated before Exportation: the profit whereof would be above 50 *per Cent.* annually to the Nation more then now it is, and is all gain'd by the *Hollanders* and *Hamburgers*, who Refine Our Mufcovado Sugar in their

Countrys cheaper by the draw back upon Mufcovado's than we can; So that they underfell us in all Forreign Markets in our own Commodity, moft of the Sugar fpent in *Germany*, *France*, and other Nations being Refined; The profit of which Meliorating as well as the Navigation being loft to the Kingdom: And it is as reafonable to fuffer Wooll to go out unmanufactur'd as Mufcovado Sugar. But more of this when I come to propofe the Method for preferving the Collonies, and this fhall likewife fuffice to explain the Nature and produce of a Sugar Plantation.

Thus it appears by all that has been fpoken of a Sugar-Plantation, that the firft coft befides the labour, skill, Care, and Induftry amounts to Five Thoufand Six Hundred Twenty Five pound. And that the produce thereof at the prefent ufuall price Currant of Sugar amounts not to Five hundred and Forty pound; out of which Deduct the conftant charge One hundred and Fifty pound, *per Annum*, the yearly value is Three hundred and inety pound, which is not 7 *per Cent*. for his Money, and yet this neither is not certain to arife. The making of Sugars, and fitting them for Market being Subject to many Contingencies more then are fet down in the Hiftory before-going; For the Plants in the ground are very often fubject to be devoured, wounded, and torn by Aunts, or undermined and deftroy'd at the Roots by Mugworms. Too much Rain, or too much Drought, in either Seafon, is a certain Diminution of the Crop, if not a totall Deftruction of the Plants; nay, if the Rains come too late, which often happens, a whole years planting is loft: when all thefe Mifchiefs are efcaped, and the Canes of a confiderable heighth, then are they liable to be twifted, broke, and totally fpoyl'd by the furious Hurricanes, that once in Three or Four years like a Fit of an Ague fhakes the whole Iflands, not only does the Crops an Injury, but fometimes tumbles down and Levells their Mills, Work-Houfes, and ftrongeft Buildings; But efcaping all thefe, as the Canes ripen they grow more and more Combuftible, and are thereby Subject to the Malice and Drunken Rages of Angry and defperate run-a way Negroes, as well as fo many other Accidents of Fire; The fury whereof when once got into a Field of Canes, is extreamly quick, terrible and fcarcely to be refifted before it has deftroy'd the whole parcell; But when they are brought to full perfection for Cutting, and the Planters expectation as ripe as they,

they, if unseasonable Rains happen, or that no winds blow, then do they all Rot and Perish on the Ground : The Slaves and Servants all stand Idle looking upon their Masters decaying Fortune, and at last are only Employ'd in clearing the Ground again from that useless Rubbish in which all that years hope is perished : Not to mention after all these mischiefs under which most Planters have many times smarted, all those Accidents, or Storms and Pirates in bringing their Commodity to Market, nor which is worst of all, their loss by breaking Customers, who not only run away with all their Produce, but with the Freight, Factoridge, and Customs, which has been paid for those Sugars they were trusted with, thereby subjecting the Industrious Planter to new and unforeseen debts and Interest for them, from whence he expected the reward of all his Labour : Nay, besides all has been said, sometimes diseases amongst Slaves and Cattell, will in a very short time sweep away a whole years Profit, besides the Constant Charge of recruiting the Natural decay of all living Creatures.

Cotton is a Commodity of great Value, and the planting it of mighty Advantage to the Common-wealth, because we have it thereby ⅔ price less then formerly, when we Imported it from Forreign parts : Its uses are too many to be Enumerated in the short Method I have proposed, Let it suffice therefore to say, that the Spinning, Weaving, and working it into Fustians, Dymitties, and many other usefull Stuffs, besides what is spent in Candles, Employs a Multitude of hands, and gains the Nation annually.

The manner of Planting it is thus A hundred Acres of Land clear'd and kept for a Cotton-Plantation requires Fifty hands, whereof Five must be White Men-Servants for the benefit of the Militia, otherwise all but two might be Black Slaves.

It is planted in Rows as our *London*-Gardners set their Damask Roses to make money of them, and rises to much about the same heighth in one year, and some few months time after its seeds are put into the Ground, which is to be done in the wet Season, when Sugar-Canes are Planting ; but sometimes it begins sooner, or later, according to the Judgment of the Experienc't Overseer ? But the same hands Employ'd in Sugar can never be Employ'd in Planting and gathering the Cotton, for when it is ripe, and the little Bags it is Contained in are Opening, it is a constant Labour

and

(22)

and Attendance from Morning to Night for the Servants to go to and again in the Intervalls between the Rows its Planted in, to take them at a Critical time, Otherwife it immediately dammages.

There are two forts of it called Ravell or Vine, that is Yellow or White, the yellow is generally efteem'd the largeft Staple.

An Acre of ground Planted therewith may produce from Four hundred to Two hundred pound weight according as it hits, So that a hundred Acres well look'd after may produce Thirty Thoufand pound weight of Cotton, which at 6d. a pound as it may yield, amounts to 150l.

Ginger is a ufefull Spice for many things, and in feveral Cafes fo Anfwers the End of Pepper, that it is obferv'd to rife and fall as that does.

It's planted by taking fmall pieces from the great Races, and placing them orderly in Trenches or Holes, as our Gardners plant Peafe, and it is done in the fame Seafons that they plant Sugar-Canes.

An Acre of Right Ground well planted will produce Two thoufand pound weight of *Ginger*, which by its Bulk in *Englifh* Tonnage, is accounted 2 Tons at leaft.

A hundred Acres requires Seventy Five hands be they Black or White Servants, but there muft by the Laws always be a fufficient Number of White-Men-Servants in proportion to the Black-flaves, otherwife all Blacks would ferve, which is much Cheaper then the Other.

I have not fet down all the Cafualties *Cotton* and *Ginger*-Plantations are fubject to, for fear of fwelling my Treatife beyond its defigned Bulk, therefore let it fuffice to fay, they are fubject to many, tho' not the fame Cafualties, both from the Alteration of Seafons and other Matters as Sugars are.

Indico is more produced in *Jamaica* than in any other Collony by reafon of the great quantity of *Savanna*-Lands there, for it thrives beft in light Sandy ground, fuch as thofe *Savanna*'s or great Plains be: The feed of it from whence it is raifed is Yellow, and round, fomething lefs than a Fitch or Tare, The ground being made light by Hoeing Trenches are made therein, like thofe our Gardeners prepare for Peafe, in which the feed is put about *March*, which grows ripe in eight weeks time, and in frefh broken ground will

Spire

Spire up to about three Foot high, but in others not more than Eighteen Inches, the stalk is full of Leaves of a deep Green colour, and will from its first Sowing yield Nine Crops in one year : when it is ripe they cut it and in proportionable Fats steep it twenty-four hours, then they clear it from the first water, and put it into proper Cisterns, where it is carefully beaten, and then is permitted to settle about eighteen hours : In these Cisterns are several Taps which let the clear water run out, and the Thick is put into Linnen-Bags of about three foot long and half a foot wide, made commonly of *Ozenbrig*-Cloath, which being hang'd up, all the liquid part drips away : When it will drip no longer it is put into Wooden Boxes about three foot long and fourteen Inches wide, and an Inch and a half deep : These boxes they place in the Sun till it grows too hot, and then take them in till the extream heat is over, continuing thus to do till it is sufficiently Dry : In Land that proves proper for *Indico*, the Labour of one hand in a years time may produce between eighty and an hundred pound weight, which may amount from twelve to fifteen pound *per annum*, to the Planter, if no accident happen : For *Indico* as well as all other Commodities of those parts is subject to many, those most common to it are Blasting and worms, to which it is very Subject.

Cacoa is now no longer a Commodity to be regarded in our Collonies, tho' at first it was the principall Invitation to the peopling *Jamaica* : For those walks the *Spaniards* left behind them there, when we Conquer'd it, produc'd such prodigious profit with little trouble that Sr. *Thomas Muddiford* and severall others set up their rests to grow wealthy therein, and fell to Planting much of it, which the *Spanish* Slaves who remained in the Island always foretold it would never Thrive, and so it happen'd ; for tho' it promised fair and throve finely for five or six years, yet still at that Age when so long Hopes and Care had been wasted about it, wither'd and Dy'd away, by some unaccountable Cause ; tho' they impute it to a Black-Worm or Grub which they find clinging to its Root. The manner of planting it is in Order like our Cherry-Gardens, which Tree when grown up it much resembles : It delights in shade, so that by every Tree they place one of *Plantain*, which produces a fruit nourishing and wholesome for their Negro's : they by Hoeing and weeding keep their *Cacoa* walks clear from Grass
continually,

continually, and it begins to bear at three, four or five years old, and did it not allmoft conftantly Dye before, would come to perfection at fifteen years growth, and laft till thirty, thereby becoming the moft profitable Tree in the World, there having been above two hundred pound *Sterling* made in one year of an Acre of it: But the old Trees planted by the *Spaniards* being gone by age, and few new thriving, as the *Spanish Negro's* foretold, little or none now is produc'd worthy the care and pains in planting and expecting it. Thofe Slaves give a Superftitious Reafon for its not Thriving, many Religious rites being perform'd at its Planting by the *Spaniards*, which their Slaves were not permitted to fee: But it is probable, that wary Nation as they remov'd the art of making *Cocheaneal*, and Curing *Venelloes* into their Inland-Provinces which were the Commodities of thofe Iflands in the *Indians* time, and forbad the opening of any Mines in them for fear fome Maritime Nation might thereby be Invited to the Conquering them, fo they might likewife in their tranfplanting *Cacoa* from the *Caracus* and *Guatemala* conceal willfully fome fecret in its planting from their Slaves, left it might teach them to fet up for themfelves, by being able to produce a Commodity of fuch excellent ufe for the fupport of mans life, with which alone and water fome perfons have been neceffitated to live 10 weeks together without finding the leaft diminution of either Health or Strength: But tho' much more might be faid yet this fhall fuffice for the Hiftory of *Cacoa* with this addition only, that it grows on the Trees in Bags or Cods of Greenifh, Red, or Yellow Colours, every Cod having in it three, four, or five Kernells about the bignefs and fhape of fmall Chefnuts, which are feparated from each other by a very pleafant refrefhing white fubftance, about the confiftence of the Pulp of a Roafted Apple, moderately fharp and Sweet, from which when Ripe it's Nuts are Separated, and by Drying Cured.

Piemento is another naturall production of thofe Iflands, but principally in *Jamaica*, from whence many call it *Jamaica-*Pepper, from the place and Figure of it; the Trees that bear it are generally very Tall and fpreading, fo that the trouble of Climbing them to gather it, would make it incredibly Dear, and thofe that be left generally growing in the Ifland, Mountains and Woods which are not taken up for Planting, but remain in the Kings hands:

Their

Their way is to go with their Slaves into the Woods where it is plenty, and cutting down the Trees, pick it off from the Branches, so that no *Piemento* comes into *Europe* twice from one Tree ; and it hap'ning often to miss for two or three years together, what it produces at present must be accounted an Accidental benefit to the Planters rather than any thing to be rely'd on as a National Advantage or constant Encouragement.

The like may be said of *Lignum Vitæ*, or *Guaiacum*, of Red-wood, and several sorts of other Trees, which come thence, for the more come the less remains, and the time required for the growing of those hard woods in the Room of those cut down, is in humane reason so many hundreds of years, that the proposing to plant them would be rather a proof of madness then foresight ; it being observable, that in those spreading woods where never Axe was handled for Cutting them down, nor Carriage came to remove them, nor Fire to burn them, there cannot be found one Dotard or perishing Tree of any usefull kind, if of any at all.

To make and manage a *Virginia* or *Maryland* Plantation for Tobacco, every hand employ'd therein must be furnisht with an Axe, a Saw, and other Instruments for felling Timber, and grubbing up its Roots.

When the ground is clear'd of Trees and Rubbish, then it is broke up with Hoes, and afterwards with those, and Spades brought into little Hillocks, like those moles turn up, into every one of which is placed one Plant, so that they grow about three, four, and five foot asunder.

The *Tobacco* Plants are rais'd from its seed sowed in Nurseries of hot beds skillfully prepar'd for that purpose in the months of *January*, *February*, *March*, and *April*, and is drawn thence and planted in the prepared little Hills in the Months of *May* and *June*, and will be ready for Cutting in *July*, or *August* following : But all the while from its planting, it is carefully to be watched, and every plant that is perceived to be dying must be taken away, and a fresh one set in the Hill, from whence the dead or dying plant was remov'd.

Tobacco Plants are very subject to be undermined, eaten and Destroy'd by a Grub or Worm that breeds about its root, which sometimes in spite of all the Care and skill of the most ingenious

E Planter

Planter will deftroy his whole Crop, nor do they ever efcape fome mifchief from it, fo that a *Tobacco* Plantation from *January,* that they fow the Seed till *Auguft*, that they Cut it, is a continuall Care and Field-labour, in Sowing, Planting, Hoeing, Weeding, Worming, Succouring, and renewing; it has feverall accidents attend it, till it be Cut and Carryed into the Curing-houfe, where it is hang'd Plant by Plant at an equall diftance till it become powder-Dry; at which time of the year that Country is fubject to great Fogs and Mifts which makes it become Waxy, and if it rifes again, then it is fully Cured, and become fit to be Casked; all Sweet-Sented requires about three weeks time, and *Orronocko* about fix weeks time; and in about three weeks time more after its Casking, it fhows it felf whether it be well Cured or no: For tho' the Experienc'd Planter knows certainly whether his *Tobacco* be well or ill-Cured, the Purchafer cannot, and may be wrong'd, if he buys it in lefs than three weeks time after its Casking: For if it had not been perfectly Dryed, it will certainly Rot, Perifh, and become good for nothing: So that not only the prime Coft but the freight home may be loft: And this the neceffities of the Planters fometimes only Occafions, for by making too much haft not to lofe his Market, many times the whole years Labour and Expectation is totally loft, And the Care therein is very great, for there is not a Leaf of *Tobacco* put on Board the Ship that is well Cured, but has pafs'd at leaft fix and thirty times through the hand of the Planter or Labourer: They fhip it out from the Month of *October* till *Aprill* following; The Annuall Exportation from all the *Tobacco-Collonies* being an Hundred and Forty Thoufand Hogfheads at four hundred and fifty pound weight to a Hogfhead.

    The Plantations are generally made into fmall parcells, not above eight or ten hands at a place, being the moft beneficiall and true way both for making the *Tobacco,* and raifing provifions for them, and the Curing-houfe muft not be at Diftance from the grounds where the *Tobacco* grows.

    The price of every pound weight of *Tobacco* Imported into the Nation before we Planted it, was from about four Shillings to fixteen Shillings a pound, and now the beft *Virginia* is not above fevenpence to the Merchant, of which the King has five pence.

    Two thirds of the *Tobacco* brought from thofe Collonies is Exported

ported to Forreign Markets, which at about three pound the Hogshead (which is the least the Nation gets by it) amounts to above two hundred thousand pound, besides the great quantity of Shipping it Employs.

It is not so little as a Million the Kingdom saves yearly by our planting *Tobacco*, so that reckoning the white people in our *Tobacco-Collonies* to be a hundred thousand Men, Women, and Children, they one with another are each of them twelve pound a year profit to the Nation.

There are in those Collonies by a probable Computation about six hundred thousand *Negro's* and *Indians*, Men, Women, and Children, and would be more, could they readyly get *Negro's* from *Guinea*, every one of which Consumes yearly two Hilling Hoes, two Weeding-Hoes, two Grubbing-Hoes, besides *Axes*, *Saws*, *Wimbles*, *Nails*, and other Iron *Tools* and *Materialls*, Consumed in Building and other Uses, to the Value of at least a hundred and twenty Thousand pound *Sterling* in only Iron-work.

The Cloaths, Guns, Cordage, Anchors, Sails and Materials for Shipping, besides Beds and other Houshold-Goods consumed and used by them, are Infinite, nor is the benefit of them to the Kingdom sufficiently to be Explain'd ; Therefore let it suffice in one word to say, that the produce and Consumption with the Shipping they give Employment to, is of an Infinite deal more benefit to the Wealth, Honour, and Strength of the Nation, then four times the same Number of Hands the best Employ'd at Home can be.

And thus much more I shall say for the Collonies, as they are to the Nation the most usefull and profitable Hands Employ'd, and the best Trade we have, both to the Consuming the Woolen-Manufactory of *England*, and the Encouraging of Navigation, So those that go thither as Servants, if they are Industrious and Just to their Masters, they live much easier than in *England*, and much more likelier to get Estates, of which there are many Presidents, and also they have been a great relief to many Men (whose misfortunes has forc'd them then to leave their own Country,) by their Carrying thither the remains of their Shipwrackt Fortunes, have recover'd their lost Estate, and very much conduced to that Increase of Wealth to this Nation as well as to the Increase of Shipping.

Shipping, which are the only true Bullworks of this Nation.

That the Courteous Reader may readily see the benefit to *England* the hands Employ'd in the Collonies are, I have here made in the nature of a Table what 50 *Negroes* with some few white hands (which are rather for security than otherwise) can make, what Tonnage, what value it produces in *England,* what Custom it pays to his Majesty, It is to be understood that all they produce is clear gains to *England* (except some Linnen, Wines and Brandy which is brought from Forreign Markets) The rest is either Freight, Custom, charges of Merchandise, Apparel, and necessaries for the Plantations or in Cash, which either serves to support the Planters when in *England,* or is laid out in purchasing Lands ; besides this, the Employing of such a vast number of Shipping and Seamen, the benefit of which is well known to every English Man. And since the Plantations have been brought to this Perfection, the Consumption of *England* saves at least two thirds by the Abatement of the price those Commodities bore before they made them, for which they never draw from *England* Gold or Silver, but on the contrary, by Exportation of what is there made over and above our Consumption, does either occasion the Enriching of *England* by monies brought from Forreign parts, for the sales of their product, or by Bartering for other Goods which must have been purchased by monies, or we must have been without them, by the hands Imployed in those Collonies Forreign Commodities became Native to the great Enriching of *England,* as aforesaid, and to the lessening the Riches and Strength of all other *European* Nations that produces the like Commodities.

An

An Account of what Advantage hands Employ'd in the Collonies are to this Nation per Annum.

	White Men.	Blacks.	Will make	which is in English Tonnage.	Value in England.	Pays Custome.
			C.			
Of Sugar.	10	50	800	40	at 20s. per C. is 800l.	at 4s. 10d. per C. is 193l. 6s. 8d.
Of Mellasses.			280	14	at 8s. per C. is 112l.	at 0s. 9d. per C. is 10l. 10s. 0.
The Excise of Mellasses when made into Spirits.						at 0s. 6d. per Gall. is 56l. 0. 0.
Totall.	10	50	1080	54	912l.	259l. 16s. 8d.
			L.			
Cotton.	5	50	33000	41¼	at 0s. 6d per l. is 785l.	at 1s. 0d. per C. is 6l. 14s. 0d.
Ginger.	5	50	15000	7½	at 20s. per C. is 134l.	at 5s. 0d. per C. is 13l. 15s. 0.
Indico.	5	50	5500	23	at 4s. per l. is 1100l.	20l. 19s. 0.
Totall.	15	150	53500	71¾	2019l.	
			C.			
Tobacco sweet scented	21	50	1430	143	at 7d. per l. is 4689l.	at 5d. per l. is 3340l. 5s. 0.
Orronocko.	21	50	1712	214	at 5d. per l. is 3954l.	at 2½d. per l. is 395l. 7s. 0.
Totall.	42	100	3142	357	8643l.	3735l. 12s. 0.

CAP. III.

From what has been said of the Nature and manner of Managing Plantations, is Demonstrated beyond all Scruple, that those Hands Imploy'd in our Collonies are for their Number the most profitable Subjects of these Dominions as well to the ends of Consumption and Delight, as for Increasing the Wealth, Power, and Glory of the Nation.

These apparent Truths being once known to and generally allow'd of by our Nobillity and Gentry, it is senceless to Imagine their could be one man amongst all our Legislators should be so malicious to the Kingdom as to desire or endeavour the Discouragement, much less Ruine of such usefull Subjects as the Planters are. But for want of Experience in, or Intelligence of their manner of Living, and Employing themselves in Plantations, the best meaning and most upright Patriots and Lovers of their Country by wrong application of that right Maxim-People, are the Riches of a Nation, may be most apt to study Restraints, Impositions, and Severities on their Trade and Negotiation, to their present Discouragement, and future Ruine : Which having in some Degree happen'd allready is the only cause I have used my Endeavours for clearing those generall Mistakes, and for laying down some few usefull Rules for the support and Encouragement of them all, but especially the Sugar-Plantations, in whose happiness I being most at present Concern'd, think my self most oblig'd to be Serviceable to my Power, as well as to clear my Reputation ; which amongst other well-meaning Gentlemen is reflected on for designing a Common Factory for keeping up the Price of their Product, and a Joynt Stock of Moneys to supply at Common Interest every Industrious Planters wants, till his Commodity could be Sold, which when rightly understood, must force forgiveness, if not Applause from the most partiall opposer of the Design.

The

The better to clear which Points, it is necessary to Obviate That, the Discouragements the Sugar-Plantations lye under, hath for three years last past furnished matters of Complaint to all persons Concern'd in that Commodity, as well Planter as Merchant, as is Evident by the Solemn Addresses were made to the Court on that Subject since the passing the Act, which lays an Additional Duty upon Sugar.

The Decay of those Collonies being granted by all parties Concern'd in that advantageous Negotiation, it will be necessary to be certain of the Cause before proper Remedies can be found out, much less apply'd to that Increasing Distemper.

For tho' in gross it may be Concluded, that the Additionall Duty occasion'd the mischief, yet those who contriv'd that Revenue for the Crown, did not intend the Burden thereof should have fallen on the Planter or Merchant, but on the Consumptioner, which then had not been the least Inconvenience or Discouragement either to Planting or Trade, and Consequently a more Equall and less Mischievous Tax could not have been laid upon the Nation.

But the price of Sugar before the Act, Compar'd with that since, and the Generall fall of Plantations, demonstrates beyond Contradiction or dispute, that the whole Burden falls on the most Industrious, most usefull, and best Employ'd People, for their Numbers can be found in all his Majesties Dominions, which are those of the Sugar Collonies, besides the Inequality of the thing, That Sixty Thousand Industrious People which the Parliament intended should pay nothing, are by Accident made to bear an Imposition design'd to be laid on the Voluntary Consumption of Eight Millions

That the matter of Fact is this, it cannot be deny'd by the most partiall and Interested, against what has been prepos'd for the Common Factory, tho' the natural aversion most Men have to new Invention, joyn'd with the private Interest of some few Men who are Factors at home, laziness of thought in some, and weakness of Understanding in others, will, I am sensible, make it difficult, if not Impossible to Establish the most Compendious and proper Remedy for that lingring distemper.

But this I dare boldly affirm, that what was then prescrib'd, carryed along with its self, Evident proofs of its Innocency and
well

well-meaning, since nothing therein could possibly take effect untill every severall Sugar-Collony in *America* had in their generall Assemblies consider'd and approv'd every part of it.

For without the Sanction and Laws of every Severall and individuall Collony, by their Acts of Assembly, the whole and every part of the Proposall was utterly inconsistent and unpracticable, as those who will give themselves leave to examine it, will undeniably find.

So that if it may be suppos'd, that the Collonies themselves are proper Judges of what they suffer, want, and would have, it cannot be deny'd, but that their minds must best appear in generall Assemblies.

From whence it consequently follows, That tho' the Proposition might not be practicable, by reason of the many different Interests it was to unite, yet that the proposers were Innocent, and Sacrificed their Labour, Expences, and Time, with a Laudable Intention.

To leave therefore that Matter in the State it is, I will proceed to Obviate the true and genuine Causes of the present Discouragements those Collonies lye under, which may be reduc'd to three Generall Heads.

1. That which is necessary to the beginning, Increase, and support of a Plantation, comes to them much dearer than it might.

2. That what they produce by Planting, is forc't to be sold at Market, much Cheaper than can be afforded to the Nations Loss as well as theirs.

3. That what they produce is Carryed to Forreign Markets at a much greater Charge than they might Carry it for.

To make it Evident, that what they want to Begin, Increase, and Support a Plantation, comes to them much Dearer than it might, I must desire the Reader to consider from what has been said concerning a Sugar Plantation, that the main support of that as well as all other Wealth is Labourers; That these Labourers in Plantations are either White Servants or Black Slaves, That the White Servants are either such as are Hired for Wages, or Assign'd for a Term of Years: Now if it appears that in the present Method all these severall sorts of Labourers come to the Planter one Third Dearer than they need, Then it must follow, that there is a burden on that Imployment as heavy, as if above thirty *Per Cent*, were laid by way of Tax upon their whole Induſtry.

That the Caſe of moſt Planters is this as well in White Servants as Slaves, and alſo in moſt of the Tools, and neceſſaries, for managing a Plantation is too much felt, to be doubted by all that are Concern'd in that Trade, or are Experienc't in Planting: But to make it clear to others, I muſt beg them to Conſider, that few men leave their Native Country willingly, who have enough conveniently to ſupport themſelves in it, except carried away by Ambition or immoderate Avarice, two paſſions little known or practis'd in *America*.

That therefore thoſe who generally go thither comply with ſome urgent preſſure in their Fortunes or Circumſtances at home, So that let them carry with them as good Underſtandings or ſtrong *Genius*'s and Inclinations to Planting as is poſſible, yet they muſt not hope to Reap without they Sow, and Wheat or any other ſort of Grain is not a more neceſſar, Seed for its own Species than Wealth is Seed to Wealth: The *Spaniards* have a Proverb to that purpoſe, which ſays, He that will bring the *Indies* home muſt Carry the *Indies* thither. It will not be unneceſſary to Explain the generall Cauſes of their firſt Thriving, that the unexperienc't Reader may have a juſt Idea of the Conveniences and Inconveniences have attended thoſe places by the many Changes have hap'ned in the Government and Laws of this Kingdom, ſince the beginning of the late Civill Wars.

To do which, we will make a ſhort reflection on the unaccountable Negligence, or rather Stupidity of this Nation during the Reign of *Henry* the Seventh, *Henry* the Eight, *Edward* the Sixth & *Queen Mary*, who could contentedly ſit ſtill and ſee the *Spaniards* Rifle, Plunder, and bring home undiſturb'd all the wealth of that Golden World; and to ſuffer them with Forts and Caſtles to ſhut up the Doors and Entrances into all the Rich Provinces of *America*, having not the leaſt Title or pretence of Right, beyond any other Nation, Except that of being by Accident the firſt Diſcoverers of ſome parts of it, where the Unpreſidented Cruelties, Exorbitances and Barbarities, their own Hiſtories witneſs, they practiſed on a Poor Naked and Innocent People which Inhabited the Iſlands, as well as upon thoſe truly Civiliz'd and mighty Empires of *Peru* and *Mexico*,

Mexico, Call'd to all mankind for Succour and Relief againſt their Outrageous Avarice and horrid Maſſacres: Therefore for a Nation Scituated like ours for Trade and Navigation, being by the Kingdom of *Ireland* the neareſt Eaſtern Neighbour to that Weſtern World: To ſit ſtill and look upon all this, without either Envy or Pitty, muſt I ſay remain a laſting Mark of the inſenſibility of thoſe Times, and the little knowledge our Forefathers had of the true Intereſt of Mankind in generall, or of their own Country in particular.

Nor did we awake from this Lethargy and wonderfull Doſing by any prudent foreſight or form'd Councill and Deſign, But ſlept on untill the Ambitious *Spaniard* by that inexhauſtible Spring of Treaſure had Corrupted moſt of the Courts and Senates of *Europe*, and had ſet on Fire by Civill Broyls and Diſcords all our Neighbour-Nations, or had ſubdued them to his Yoak, Contriving too, to make Us wear his Chains, and bear a ſhare in the Triumph of Univerſall Monarchy, not only Projected, but near accompliſh't when Queen *Elizabeth* came to the Crown, as all Hiſtorians of thoſe times do plainly make appear: And to the divided Intereſts of *Phillip* the Second, and Queen *Elizabeth* in perſonall more than Nationall Concerns, we do owe that ſtart of hers in letting looſe upon him, and Encouraging thoſe daring adventurers *Drake, Hawkyns, Rawleigh*, the Lord *Clifford*, and many other Braves that Age produced; who by their Privateering and bold undertaking, like thoſe the *Buccaneers* practiſe, now open'd the way to our Diſcoveries and Succeeding Settlements in *America*; which ſince as it were by Chance, occaſion'd only by the Neceſſities of many, wrought upon by the Example, Wiſdom, and Succeſs of ſome few particulars, without any form'd Deſign, Help or Aſſiſtance from our State-Councells, or Legiſlators, in leſs then one Century, hath Throve ſo well, that they are become the Example and Envy, and might be the Terrour of all our Neighbour Maritime Nations: And do undoubtedly Maintain above half that vaſt quantity of Shipping we Employ in Forreign Trade; ſo that it can be from no other cauſe but want of Information that many of our Laws as well as Court-Maxims and Practices, run oppoſit to their Encouragement, Protection, and Increaſe.

The beginning of our *American* Settlements were made in the latter

latter end of Queen *Elizabeths* Reign, by the Encouragement of Sr. *Walter Rowleigh*, who undertook the Planting of *Virginia*, and first brought the use of *Tobacco* into *England*; but that nor any other Collony of ours in the *West-Indies* did promise much Success either to the Nation or Undertakers, untill the Reign of King *James the first*, whose Peace with the Crown of *Spain* restrain'd those bold Privateers who before by Harasing the *Spanish* Collonies and Mast'ring their Rich Ships of Plate, had become very Wealthy as well as Numerous: But much against the will of most of them, but Principally of such who had not sufficiently made their fortunes, this Peace oblig'd them to change the prospect of their future Conduct from Rapine and spoyl, to Trade and Planting; So that in a very short time a considerable Settlement was made in the Northern parts of *America*, to the great Increase of good Shipping in the Kingdom: By this means a generall Notion of having enough profitable Land in those parts of the world for nothing, so infected the whole Kingdom, that not only the Necessitous and Loose part of the Nation flockt thither, but many Non-conformists did Solicite his Majesty for leave to make a Settlement together under priviledges and Liberties, both in Civil and Church-Matters, by a Constitution of their own. This Combination King *James* prudently consented to, and Confirm'd by his Letters-Patents, wisely foreseeing, that tho' a *Species* of a Commonwealth was thereby introduc'd into his Dominions, yet the dependence thereof must be upon the Crown for protection, and consequently that part of his Subjects then call'd Puritans, would not be totally lost to the Nation, as they must be if driven for ever to remain in Forreign Countryes: Thus began that Numerous Collony of *New-England*, where under frugall Laws, Customs and Constitutions, they live, without applying themselves to Planting any *Tobacco* or other *American* Commodities, except for their own private use. But by Tillage, Pasture, Fishing, Manufactures and Trade, they to all Intents and purposes imitate old *England*, and did formerly much, and in some Degree do now Supply the other Collonies with Provisions in Exchange for their Commodities, as *Tobacco, Sugar, &c.* which they carried to Forreign Markets, how conveniently for the Nations Interest I shall not determine, being no Enemy to any kind of honest Industry: But this cannot chuse but be allow'd, that if any

F 2   hands

hands in the *Indies* be wrong Employ'd for Domeſtick Intereſt, it muſt be theirs, and thoſe other Collonies, which ſettle with no other proſpect than the like way of Living: Therefore if any ſuch only ſhould be neglected and diſcourag'd who purſue a Method, rivalls our Native Kingdom, and threatens in time a totall Independency thereupon.

But as this cannot be ſaid of our *Tobacco*-Collonies, much leſs it is to be fear'd from our Sugar-Plantations, except by groſs miſtakes at home we at laſt force them to part with their black-Slaves to the *Spaniards*, and betake themſelves to the ſole Planting of Proviſions, and living upon their Eſtates, which ſhould it happen would be the greateſt blow to our Navigation, and conſequently to the Rents that the Kingdom ever received ſince it was a Trading Nation.

This Digreſſion I hope may be pardon'd, ſince it Explains a little the difference of our Nationall Intereſt in the ſeverall ſorts of *American* Collonies.

Nor would I be ſuppoſed to be ſo Ignorant, to think, that no kind of Collonies can Empty, and conſequently Ruine the Nation: No, there is a naturall boundary to all worldly matters; and it becomes the Wiſedom of Legiſlators truly to diſtinguiſh the depending and profitable, from the Detacht and Undermining Collonies, and rightly apply Lenitives and Corroſives accordingly.

To return therefore to thoſe within the Tropicks which are principally ſuppoſed by making Sugar; The beginning of their Settlement was without the leaſt proſpect of Succeeding in that Commodity, the Art of making which, as I ſaid before being by meer Accident gain'd in *Barbados* by a *Hollander*, ſomething more than halfa Century ſince: And as it was the happineſs of thoſe Iſlands to learn it from a *Dutchman*, ſo the firſt and main ſupporters of them in their progreſs to that perfection they are arrived to, exceeding all the Nations in the World, is principally owing to that Nation, who being eternall Prolers about, and Searchers for moderate Gains by Trade, did give credit to thoſe *Iſlanders* as well as they did to the *Portugalls* in *Braſile*, for Black Slaves, and all other neceſſaries for planting, taking as their Crops throve, the Sugar they made: Thus with light but ſure Gains to themſelves, they nouriſht the Induſtrious, and conſequently Improving Planters,

ters, both before, and during the Civill Wars in thefe Iflands: the Fame of whofe good Fortune being fpread at home, many ingenious Gentlemen who had unfortunately follow'd the Royall Intereft Convey'd the remains of their fhipwrackt Fortunes thither: amongſt which Collonell *Henry Walldronds* Father, with himſelf and other his Relations of that Family, were not inconſiderable either for Quality, Induſtry, or Parts: So that by theirs and many undone Cavaliers who follow'd their Example, new Improvements and Experiments were dayly added to the Art of Planting, making, and Refining Sugar, which were taken from them by the *Dutch* till Sir *George Askew* with a Squadron of Ships remov'd the Lord *Willoughby* of *Parham* from Governing there, for his Exill'd Majeſty *Charles the Second,* and Reduced the Iſland to the *States* Obedience: Soon after which the *Dutch War* hap'ning, all further Trade with that Nation ceaſt, by whoſe help they being then ſtrong enough to ſubſiſt of themſelves, their future Dealing return'd to its proper Center, which was Trading with their native Country; ſince which time that Iſland which contains but   Acres, and not more than five and twenty thouſand white Inhabitants, has produced in Commodiⁱies above thirty Millions *Sterling,* has pay'd in Duties to ſupport the Government at a modeſt Computation, above ¼ of a Million which will ſeem incredible to thoſe that have not Employ'd thoughts on it.

I have rather mentioned Collonel *Henry Walldrone* for one Inſtance of ſuch as our Civill War drove abroad, becauſe in his particular Caſe and Sufferings, great inferences may be made for Explaining the many Inconveniences thoſe Collonies are now Subject to, as well as becauſe he has been one who did Endeavour to Obviate the Miſchief attended the Act for additionall Duty upon Sugar, and was moſt Zealous in his Applications at Court for Relief to his fellow-Planters, even whilſt he ſtruggl d under ſuch ſevere Oppreſſions of Power as might have reduc't to Deſpair the greateſt Courage: and to him and his continuall Endeavours for their benefit, all the Planters in the *Indies* owe their Thanks at leaſt, for he not only made the Court ſenſible of the great Miſtake they lay under, both by the laying and unjuſt manner of Collecting that Additionall Duty which at leaſt will prove a caution to future Councells for their Conduct in like Caſe, But was at great Labour and Charge in Conjunction with my felf and other Gentlemen, intelligent perfons in that Affair, to invent if poffible a proper Remedy for their languifhing Condition, which can never be but by fome fuch way as may furnifh them with fufficient Money and Credit on their Induftry and Commodities, as may enable them to buy their neceffaries at reafonable Rates, and Sell their produce at a faving Price, neither of which it is poffible for them to do at prefent.

For tho' to do right to the *Affrican* Company they have been wonderfully kinde in the Credit they have given the Plantations, and that rightly managed a Company is able to fupply them with Negro's Cheaper than a loofe Trade could, yet the Complaints the Company continually make of the Collonies bad pay, and the Complaints of the Collonies for being ill fupplyed with Negro's, allow both true, it will be neceffary to Enquire into the reall caufe of both Inconveniencies before proper Remedies can be propos'd.

To ftate the Cafe truly 'tis to be confider'd that when the Company was firft Erected, with Exclufion to all others for Trading in *Guinea*, the confequence thereof was never forefeen by the Planters, for if it had, they could not have fail'd Complaining againft its Eftablifhment upon the foundation of fuch Privileges they now pretend to ; Nor could any invention in the world have appear'd a more pernicious Monopoly, than that would have been Judg'd to be upon a free Examination, before Cuftome and Neceffity had reduc'd the Collonies to a Servile Dependence thereupon.

For let be granted there was a kind of a Prudent neceffity in the Government here, to unite a Company for fecuring the Gold and Teeth Trade in *Guinea*, and that it was in the power of the Crown to prohibit all others but fuch Company, to Trade, within the Limits affign'd them by their Charter ; Yet this did not at all reach the Plantations at firft, nor did feem to prohibit them from buying Slaves at the beft Market, as fince it has been Interpreted : For with fubmiffion to better Judgments, the confequence of that Interpretation feems to me to be an Inlet to all manner of Monopolies.

For why fhould not the Crown by the fame Rule make a Company who fhould have only power to Trade thither in Iron-ware, and another for Wine, the like for Mum, or any other Commodity they want, as to prohibit bringing thither Slaves but for the Company's

Company's Account, for the Case to all intents and purposes is the same, for it is beyond all dispute known, that the Collonies under a free, Open, and Loose Trade for *Negro's*, did flourish and Increase before the Company was Erected.

It is certain, that they could still be supplied plentifully at ⅓ the price the Company makes them pay.

It is as undeniable, that the Company doth not Supply them with the full Numbers they want, and could have, did not the Company shut all doors to their Supply.

And it cannot be denied, but in these few heads are included all the several Inconveniences so Complain'd of in a Monopoly.

I. For hereby a loose Trade is turn'd into a Restrain'd, which lessens the Numbers of Shipping that would Trade to *Guinea*.

II. That comes dear to the Subject that might be Cheap.

III. And a usefull Commodity to the Increase of Wealth is not to be had in a sufficient quantity.

It is alledged that some part of the Trade of *Guinea* considering who are our Rivalls in it, cannot be preserved without Force, and that the Castle must be maintain'd or that part of the Trade lost, and that the Castle &c. cannot be supported but with great Cost, And that that charge falls extreamly heavy upon so small a stock as that of the *African* Company.

The consequence of which premises is, They will always be necessitated to keep up the price of *Negro's* ⅓ more than otherwise we need, (tho' the Castles are not supported, or little or no ways usefull to the *Negro*-Trade, they keeping no Forts, and seldom Factors at those places where the *Negro's* are most bought at.)

I confess a strong Argument for the Company, but a sowr one for the Collonies which seem hereby depriv'd of their Birthright, The Liberty of the Subject, and their possession which Consisted in a loose Trade.

The Premises considered, the Planters may therefore justly desire that the National Interest in the *Guinea*-Trade, The Forts, &c. may be equally supported by all the Nation, as our Navy's necessary Forts and Garrisons at home are, and not fall solely on their Labour and Industry: For the necessary supply of *Negro's* to the Collonies Annually should not be less than Twenty thousand pound.

Therefore upon a fair Representation of the Charge of the Caftle &c. it cannot be queftion'd but the Parliament will provide for their fupport, if it appear a National Intereft, to preferve the Collonies, and that Trade, as no doubt it is.

But as I hinted before, another caufe of their felling dear is the bad Pay they Complain of in the Collonies, and it may not be without Caufe that the Company complains : Not that the Collonies give occafion for it, as matters now ftand.

For the Country not being able to get *Negro*'s but at too dear, and *Negros*' being the main prop of a Plantation, it neceffarily follows, the Planter muft be neceffitous, and thereby forc'd to fell his produce Cheap, not being able thro' Poverty to keep his Commodity by him untill it will yield a faving price.

Thus the true caufe of his Selling Cheap, is his buying Dear, and both together keep the Induftrious Planter, who is not got aforehand in his affairs allways indigent and in Debt to the Company : This Debt being as they alledge near three hundred thoufand pound, keeps the Companies ftock, which at firft was not more than a hundred and ten thoufand allways out of their hands , The Intereft of which, with the charge of the Caftle, falling upon fo narrow a ftock as four hundred thoufand pound. This rifing at laft upon the Plantations, makes their Burden grievous at prefent, and muft at laft prove infupportable, as the Debt Increafes, for that, and their neceffities will keep pace together, except fome fpeedy Remedy be found for them both.

All this taken apart and duly confider'd, it will appear probable to all thinking men, that the Plantations muft Speedily be Ruin'd, and the Commodities fo profitable to the Nation, fluctuate into the hands of fome Neighbour-Collonies, who do not ftruggle under the like Inconveniences ; For which time the *French*, *Dutch*, *Danes*, and many other Nations are at watch, and do at prefent Increafe, proportionably to our difcouragements : In this Difmall Profpect we muft let them ftand untill we come to confider of proper Remedies for thefe and the following Inconveniences.

Another Inconvenience attends them, proceeds from the wrong Notion which has infected our Judges, as well as the lefs intelligent Gentry, that the People which go thither are a Lofs to the Nation.

This, with fome other more Malicious, but as weak Suggeftions

ons, has occasion'd severe and terrible Sentences about Exporting white Servants on pretence of Spiriting, so that many have been forc'd to send for those who have been Transported thither to produce again before the Judges to acknowledge their voluntary Transportation.

This Occasions new Offices, new Fees, new Methods, for sending Servants thither, all which increases their price in the *Indies* very considerably, and falls as bad as a Tax on the Industry of the Planter; besides makes Servants so scarce, that a universal Languishing of such plantations as are growing happens thereby, and that want of white-Servants for term of years occasions the Increase of wages to those they are forc'd to Hire at great Rates to Supply that Defect: This Increase of wages is not only a new Burden upon the present Planters, but lessens their Numbers, many choosing rather to sell their Industry and Labour, to support themselves under others, than begin planting themselves under such visible Incumbrances as dayly Increase upon that Employment.

Thus one Inconveniency begets another to the Ruine of the present, and discouragement of future Planting, which before I have done must more and more appear as National a concern as any our Council can be busied about.

It is true, many of the first comers, especially in *Barbados* are got above the danger of Ruine by these and other following mischief, that dayly must, if not prevented, Increase upon all who are not in the like Circumstance for Wealth, and peradventure to such the prospect of this General Decay promises a good return and recompence for all the Inconveniences they at present feel in the abatement of the value of their Plantations

For some of them may perhaps consider, that as the debts of the Collonies Increase to the *African* Company, the ruine of necessitous Planters must follow, as they tumble the quantity of Sugar produc'd, must diminish, and as that happens, the price must rise; So that their own Plantations being sure to stand, must likewise improve at last, proportionably to the General and National loss besides: That they are sure as Plantations, *Negro*'s and Stock come to be seiz'd for debt, they will be sold for less than their half value, and can be no Mens Money but theirs who have it to spare; That this hath and doth dayly happen, and must more and more, if no

G   Remedy

Remedy be found out, is so certain, that none Intelligent among the *American* Merchants and Factors but knows many sad Examples of that kind; So that if the price should rise by abatement of quantity, tho' convenient for some overgrown Planters and Wealthy Merchants, does tend to nothing less then the decay of Shipping, lessening the Numbers of White People, and driving them to the *Dutch* Plantations.

Another great discouragement those Collonies lye under, is the Arbitrary Power and practices of their Governours there, and the Court at home, which some have to their undoing felt and all are liable to.

I will instance in the Case of some few, that the Reader may the better Judge of the Condition of them all.

In the year 1669. Coll. since Sir *Henry Morgan* commonly called *Panama Morgan*, for his Glorious undertaking and Conquest of the *Spaniards* of that place, by fewer then Twelve hundred Men, without either Horse or Pikemen to oppose in fair fight above Six Thousand Foot, and Five hundred Horse, which he did and afterwards took and ransackt a Town, that had baffled, when not half so strong the famous Sir *Francis Drake* who attaqu'd it with Four Thousand. This Man as great an Honour to our Nation and terrour to the *Spaniards* as ever was born in it, Notwithstanding he had done nothing but by Commission of the Governour and Councill of *Jamaica*, and had received their Formal and Publick thanks for the Action, was upon a Letter from the Secretary of State sent into *England* a Prisoner, and without being Charged with any Crime, or ever brought to a Hearing, he was kept here at his own great Expence above Three year, not only to the wasting of some thousands he was then worth, and bringing him into great debts, but to the hinderance of his Planting, and Improvement of his Fortune by his Industry, towards which none in that place was in a fairer way; So that under those difficulties, and the perpetual Malice of a prevailing Court-Faction, he wasted the remaining part of his life, oppreft not only by those but by a lingring Consumption, the coldness of this Climate and his vexations had brought him into, when he was forced to stay here.

Another remarkable Example of the like Inconveniencies they have been and are liable to is, that of the beforementioned Colonel *Wallrond*,

Wallrond, who upon a bare suggestion against him made by a Man fairly tryed before a Court of *Oyer and Terminer*, wherein he was but one, tho' the first Commission, was Commanded from *Barbados* hither, where he has been detain'd above three Years, And at last upon a full Tryal at an Assizes in the Countrey where his Adversary was powerfull, and himself utterly a Stranger, there was given aginst him but 30*l* damrage, and that for no other reason, but that the Court-Judge was pleased to over-rule this Plea:—— Whereby such a Disorder, Ruine, and Distraction of his Wife, Children, Family, Plantation and Estate, has hapned to him, that as the Calamity is not to be exprest, and for some respects is not fit to be related, so it could never have been supported by any Man but one of an Extraordinary Fortitude and Understanding, which he has Demonstrated by his constant Endeavours under his unjust Oppressions to serve the Publick Int'rest of those Collonies, and rightly to represent their sad Condition at Court, especially that of *Barbados*, who was so kind and just to him at his coming thence, as by the representative body of that Island, together with his Majesties Governour and Council, to make a present unto him of Five hundred pound *Sterling* in acknowledgment of his good Service he had done that Country, together with a publick Declaration of his just proceedings in that Court of *Oyer and Terminer*, and especially in this Case, he was brought over upon; And this I must further observe to the Reader, that it was not the least Crime of State was so much as alledg'd against him, for banishing him from *Barbados* into *England*, but meerly private Malice supported by the Partiall Tyranny of some great Men occasioned all his sufferings.

I shall not mention the Numerous Examples of Men have been thus sent from their Habitation and Industry in those parts, but shall content my self with these two notorious Instances of the hard Case those well-Employ'd Members of the Nation are in, For any man who would think it destructive to Liberty and Property to be banisht into *Barbados*, *Jamaica*, or any other Collony from *England*, must believe it is as great an Oppression to be kept from thence against his will, when all his Fortune and Estate not only lies there, but for want of his own management is liable to infinite more Casualties and loss than any Estate in *England* can be.

Another Inconveniency attends the Collonies, is, their being forced

ced to bring their Commodities firſt into *England* before they can carry it to any Forreign Market, which would appear upon a true Examination, not the leaſt advantage to the Nation, but a great loſs, as I ſhall demonſtrate when I come to propoſe proper Remedies for theſe and many other Inconveniences the Collonies at preſent ſtruggle under, which might be remov'd with greater Profit both to the Crown and Kingdom than to them.

Thus in ſhort it appears, that Buying the neceſſary matters for beginning and Supporting a Plantation ¼ dearer then might in a right method be afforded them, is one great Diſcouraging to Planting.

A Second is, that ſome of them being neceſſitous, they are all forced to ſell their produce much cheaper than they can under that Burden, afford them.

A third for want of a ſufficient ſtock or Credit they are not able to Meliorate their Sugars to a degree fit for Conſumption, whereby ſo beneficiall an Art is thrown away upon our *Hamburgh* and *Holland*-Neighbours, to the mighty Increaſe of their Wealth and Navigation, by our Neglect as well as Inconvenient Cuſtoms and Laws.

A Fourth, by being Subject to the Inconveniency of Complaints, Suits, and Removals into *England* for matters ſufficiently Cognizable in thoſe parts; To all which I ſhall only add to this Section two more.

The firſt, a want of a true Method for preſerving the Eſtates and Plantations of deceaſed Perſons for the uſe of their Relations or Creditors in *England*.

And Laſtly, by the great quantity of Commodities are ſent out of the Leeward *Carribee* Iſlands, and ſold to the *Dutch* at low prices, for private Lucre, for thoſe people ſaving all the Duty as well of the 4 ½ *per Cent.* there, as the Cuſtoms in *England*, and having Goods in Barter for them directly from *Holland*, can afford their Sugar much Cheaper than their Neighbours; ſo that there goes out of that back door for *Holland* under the name St. *Euſtace* Sugar, above a Thouſand and Five hundred Hogſheads of Muſcovado Sugar, which refined with great advantage to that Nation in *Holland* keeps the Market Low in all Forreign parts; The proper Remedies for all which Inconveniences I ſhall ſtrive to propoſe in my next Chapter.

Cap. IV.

CAP. IV.

BY what has been said before, I will take it for granted, that the Reader discerns clearly how much to the advantage of the Nation all those hands are Employ'd which go to our *American* Collonies, and principally such as Transport themselves and Servants to the *Sugar*-Plantations, as likewise how many inconvenient discouragements they at present Struggle.

The first Remedy to which Inconveniences that I shall presume to Propose, is what we most certainly are very defective in for the greatest Concern of the Nation, which is for all sorts of Trade, I mean an Able Dilligent, Impartiall, and constant Sitting Councell of Trade, where all sorts of Propositions concerning it might freely be Debated, and thoroughly Examined before they come into the Parliament or Councell, for such a constitution would be an infallible Touch-stone to try the intrinsick Value of all Notions, and Projects, that mankinde can Invent, either for the generall good or particular advantage: It being allmost impossible for the Privy-Councell or Committees of Parliament in the methods they proceed by, ever to Inform themselves rightly of any one Difficult matter comes before them.

For let but a Thinking-man any ways verst in Trade but reflect, how many interferring Accidents there is belongs to that mystery, and how many various shapes every Branch of it has taken before it arriv'd to perfection, and they will conclude it impossible for Noblemen and Gentlemen by short Debates partially Manag'd, as they are usually before them, ever to arrive to a perfect Understanding of the matters in question, for want of which, their judgements are abus'd by Clamour, Importunity, Prejudice, Partiallity, or some other prevailing Byas, and seldom or never, if the matter be of Importance enough to require Debating, ever come to a right

Decision,

Decifion, whereby at laft the Secretary or Clerk to fuch a Board becomes the only Oracle to it, and as he feels the Caufe heavy or light, Weakly or PotentlyBackt, can read its Deftiny before One Argument is heard, concerning the matter in Iffue, be it of never fo confiderable Confequence.

That this is true, all men who have ever been concern'd to attend thofe kind of Affemblies, can infallibly witnefs; but withall one would wonder that a Nation fo concern'd for their Intereft as Ours, wherein there are few men, will make a Step in any Confiderable Dealing, without the advice of fome Councell Learned in the Point : That the Government of it which fhould confift of the wifeft of them, fhould take upon them to alter and change the fhape of the greateft concerns of the whole, without the Impartiall Advice of fome continually Active and Solicitous in the Miftery of it; But this being fo, it is no wonder Our Laws and Councell-Book-Orders are fo often forc'd to be chang'd, for being in direct Oppofition to a Nationall Intereft ; Therefore as the firft great Remedy to the Grievances attend Our Collonies, I do Propofe that a Councell of Trade may by Act of Parliament be Eftablifh't to confift of a Prefident, Vice-Prefident, and fome convenient number of Members who may continually be fitting to Hear, Debate, and Examine all fort of Propofalls and Difficulties that arife about Trade; and that they may have fuch Sallaries out of the publick Purfe as may make the Bufinefs worth wife mens attendance ; that no Propofall whatever fhould there be refus'd to receive a Debate and two or three hearings, or more, as the matter Imports, that nothing fhould be difmift with a refufall, but with the Reafons the Councell had for doing it, Annext to the Propofall : That no Judgment of theirs fhould be Finall or Concluding, but fubject to review either there at the Privy-Councell or Parliament, when anfwers were in Writing made and Exhibited againft fuch Reafons: And that nothing fhould be advanc'd either in Parliament or Privy-Councell that concern'd the Plantations, Forreign-Negotiation, Manufactures, Trade or Patents for new Inventions, which had not been weigh'd and examined if not approv'd of in mature Debates at that Councell when Eftablifht.

If fuch a Board as this was Erected under members of large *Genius*'s and proper Rules, it would fave me and every other Man concern'd cern'd for the publick, the pains I and they take in writing on these sort of Theams; and the Memoirs, Debates, and Resolutions of that so necessary Assembly would be the undoubted Rules for guiding all Commerce, as well as laying on of proper Impositions upon Trade: But for want of such a Court to have recourse to; I am forced to Appeal to all mankind, by a more troublesome and tedious as well as less Significant Method, which is writing a Book, which may if not lead to a Remedy for the Plantations, at least shew I design'd nothing else when I enter'd into the Undertaking I formerly mentioned.

To hasten therefore to my desired End, I would propose as one effectuall way to help the Plantations, that a sufficient Fund of money might be lodg'd there, to which as to an infallible Bank every Planter might have recourse, for credit, proportionable to the reall value of any he has to give in Security, be it Land, Stock or Goods; Now that the want of a Stock of Money in the Plantations is a great hindrance to their Increase, is plain from the great Debt due from them to the *Affrican* Company, which as it Increases does more and more make the Company incapable of sending them Sufficient Numbers of *Negro's*, at an equall and Moderate price, as it does them to pay for them when they arrive: But was there a sufficient Bank upon the Place to which every Man at the Common Interest of the place might have recourse, That Grievance would naturally End, and a Plantation like all Increasing things would thrive by having it's proper nourishment, Money.

But it is Objected, that the legall Int'rest of the *Collonies* is so high, that it gives Sufficient Encouragement to monied men to lend their Money there, without a Joynt stock or great Fund to be provided, and sent thither only for that purpose: But Experience as well as right reason Evince the Contrary, for we see and the *Affrican* Company sufficiently find, that money and Credit are the things most wanted there, notwithstanding the heighth of Interest: For tho' a man that has three or four thousand pound to put out, would be glad to have ten *Per Cent*. rather than five for it if it were equally legall and secure, yet will he not think it worth while to leave his Native Country Friends and Customary Recreations, to follow extraordinary five *Per Cent*: to the *Barbados*: Or if he did, would there lend it at Interest, but would as others do, endeavour to employ

ploy it in more profitable Ways : And to send it thither, or to any other Collony, without going himself, is too hazzardous for any prudent man to venture : But if a sufficient Joynt-Stock was United under proper Rules and Priviledges, for the Use of all the Plantations, there is no doubt but the bare Encouragement of that Extraordinary Interest would sufficiently invite Money'd men into the Society ; when without the least personall Care or possibility of hazzard their Business, must of necessity be rightly Negotiated by those proper Methods all Companies constantly take for the Common Interest of the Society : And as nothing could be of more advantage to the Collonies, than a sufficient Credit for every man that had a stock to have recourse to, so nothing could be more necessary for the publick to do for them than to Unite such a stock for their Use, which was one and the main Branches of the Undertaking, and would have answered the End of their wants, which is to Buy what they want for ready money, at reasonable Rates, which now all men know the needy Planter can no ways do.

To Compass the Second End, which is to enable the Planter to sell his Commodity at a full saving price, a Common Factory is absolutely necessary ; For whilest there are both poor and Rich men in the World, their Interests in divided Dealing must of necessity Clash ? The poor man must sell his Commodity at the price his pressing Occasions force him to comply with, and the Rich man must at last come to the same price, or never sell at all, when perhaps the Consumption of the Commodity dealt in, would not be a jot more or less for twenty *Per Cent.* difference in the price : that this is the Case in *Sugar*, *Tobacco*, and some other Plantation-Commodities is certain, so that nothing places the Duty laid by Parliament on those things to be born by the Planter, but the necessitous Seller, who must take the first Chapmans money ; Or the necessitous Factor which is all one : That this is plain they will all Confess that Opposed a Common-Factory, So I shall Expose all that Mistery, aiming more to do the Business, and Justify my own Candour ; than to anger any man Concern'd either for his reputation or profit.

Wherefore let it suffice on this head, to say, That a Common Factory if practicable and made equall, would keep up a full saving price in any Commodity whatever, as well as *Sugar* and also ſo would place any Duty the Parliament could invent on the conſumptioner, and not on the Maker or Dealer in it: And that the common-Factory intended was practicably and equally deſigned, will to every diſintereſted man appear, who will but examine the Draughts prepared to be offer'd to the Aſſemblies of the ſeverall Collonies, to whoſe Approbation or Diſlike they were abſolutely to be ſubmitted, before any Joynt-Stock could have been United for their ſervice: Nay, I dare further affirm, that no able or conſiderable Factor but muſt have found his Account by Employment in the Common-Factory, equall to his buſineſs in his particular Dealing, ſince all the perſons to be employ'd therein were allways to be nominated by the ſeverall Collonies, and to have been accountable only to the Planters for their Produce.

But leaving that matter at preſent, I do affirm, that nothing can ever keep up the Juſt price of *Sugars* and other *Weſt-India* Commodities, like an equall Common-Factory and that well ſettled would ſecure the Planter againſt all Accidents of new Impoſitions, let them be what they would, provided it is pay'd back upon Exportation, and a Proportionable advance were plac'd on the ſame Commodities coming from Foreign parts; by which as an equall Standard, the Parliament too would ſecure the Nation from being Impos'd upon by any exceſſive Price.

Another mighty benefit both to the King, Planter, and Merchant, would accrew by a Common-Factory, if the Cuſtomes and impoſitions on their Commodities were reduced to a Commutation of ſo much *Per Cent.*, upon Sales as was proportionable to them, for hereby the Importer would not be burden'd with paying down and riſqueing his Duty in truſting his Chapman, nor could the King looſe the leaſt part of what was Due to him, which conveniences were provided for by another Branch of the ſaid Undertaking.

But to paſs again from that, I ſay, nothing can enable the Planters to buy neceſſaries Cheap, like a ſufficient Bank of Credit, nor nothing keeps up the Price of the Commodity as Plantations Increaſe like a Common Factory.

In the next place, to Remedy another Inconveniency attends thoſe Plantations, which is, being forced to bring their produce firſt into *England*, before they can ſend it to Forreign Markets. But if they had the Priviledge to carry thoſe Commodities directly

rectly abroad which were fully Meliorated, free from paying any Duty or Cuftome, and Superfluous to our own Confumption, the Crown which is the great End of the conftraint could not in the leaft Suffer, & we with Profit might gain all Forreign Markets, & fet the price of thofe Commodities abroad which we cannot now do, being liable to greater charge by longer Voyages, Double Rifques, and the expence of Time and Labour, in Loading and Unloading fuch Goods, which was alfo provided for in another Branch of the faid undertaking.

To prevent the Incroachment and mifreprefentations of Governours and malicious Men againft the Induftrious Planter, Merchant and Inhabitants of thofe Collonies, Itinerate Judges might be fent Annually, fully Impower'd to Infpect, examine, and reprefent matters to the Privy-Councel at their Return ; & finally to determine any appeals from the Supream Courts and Councells there : to conftitute which Jurisdiction it might be neceffary, that three or more of the Members of the Councell of Trade, having not the leaft private Intereft or dealing in thofe Collonies, might be fent out, attended by a Regifter or Clerk of that grand affize with a man of War, firft to touch at *Barbados*, next at the *Leward Iflands*, next at *Jamaica*, then at *Carolina*, So on thro' *Virginia*, *Mary-land*, *Penfylvania*, *New-York*, and *New-England*, and fo from thence home. The Major part of them to be Parramount in all Civill cafes to all Governours, wherever they refided, that immediately on their arrivall the Affemblies fhould meet and Sit, by whom they might receive a full account of the Wants, Defects and Requefts of each place, as alfo Examine the feverall Adminiftrations of Goods belonging to perfons in *England* by the Death of Relations, and any other matters, might prevent Injuftice or the neceffity of fetching perfons thence from their Families or Bufinefs on any Complaints in *England*, that they might be obliged to hold a fort of a Term for three weeks before fetting Out to receive Oaths of Witneffes to be ufed in Evidences there, as alfo pretences to Eftates of perfons Deceafed, and Controverfies about Bills of Exchange, or any other matters which occafion Delay now, and difcourages Dealing in thofe parts; That none of thofe Judges fhould go two years Succeffively together, but that a Rotation of that Employment as near as may be, fhould be appointed amongft the members which

Compofed

(51)

Compofed the Councell of Trade; That they fhould have fufficient Salleries for their Trouble, and not be fuffered to receive any other Fee, Prefent, or Reward, befides Meat and Drink, whatever an Infinite number of Conveniencies might arife to thofe Plantations by fuch a laft Refort: The manner as well as the full Jurisdiction I will omit, being neceffary to be more enlarged upon, than I am willing in the fhort Method I have propofed to my felf.

In the next place, I cannot chufe but think that the Judges after fuch a Court was Eftablifht, might omit taking Cognizance of thofe Malicious and troublefome, rather then neceffary Complaints, about carrying People to the *Indies*, any man concern'd being there upon the place able to make his complaint, and receive full damages for any abufe put upon him for an unvoluntary Tranfportation or Non performance of the Contract made with them: This would open the Gap to many Peoples going thither, than which I have proved nothing can be of more advantage to the Commonwealth, fo that by faving many troublefome Fees, and other Dangers, in fending White-Servants, they might be had much cheaper by the Planter to his great Encouragement.

In the next place, begging pardon of the *African* Company, if I err, I cannot fee an honeft Reafon why the Planters fhould not be at full Liberty to buy Blacks at the beft Market they can, the act of Navigation preferved; For is their Patent alone a fufficient Juftification to fo perfect and mifchievous a Monopoly as that Inhibition they pretend to feems to be? For tho' they may give many Reafons to Warrant that United Stock and Sole Trading in *Guinea* to them, yet I cannot fee that can hinder Black-Slaves to be brought to the Plantations by any *Englifh* Ship from any other place: But this I am fure of, that fince they may be had by private Merchants ⅓ cheaper than the Company will afford them, they ought to be at Liberty to have them fince the Nation is ten times more gainer by the labour of the Blacks than the Company is by their Price, and ⅓ more of Blacks Employ'd in Planting, which would follow, if they were ⅓ cheaper, which would alfo enable them to fell the produce of the Colonies cheaper, by which means they would be able to ruine all other Forreign Collonies; and in time we may by cheap felling get the whole Trade of Sugar into our Hands,

H 2   which

which muſt be ſuch a National profit by this, and our Former Computations, that no Argument on the other ſide for the Companies' Intereſt can in the leaſt Ballance: Beſides, if it ſhould be allow'd, that the Company furniſhes the *Sugar Collonies* with more than they are well payd for, at the Price they take yet they do not bring them in all ⅓ ſo many as they could Employ, and do furniſh the *Tobacco* Plantations with none at all (except what are firſt agree'd for in *England*, and then the Merchant pays Extravagantly, and the Planter muſt advance for the Merchants Encouragement, ſo muſt pay a double profit,) who would if they had them at a moderate price quickly double their Numbers to a mighty Increaſe of Shipping and Nationall Wealth; Thus the prohibition and totall Ingroſſing the Trade of Blacks by the Company, does ſeverail ways infinitely prejudice the Plantations and induſtrious Planters in them, as well as prejudice the Publick; But if the preſervation of the *Guinea* Trade be of ſuch advantage to the Kingdom, that the Caſtles muſt be maintain'd, it is but reaſonable thoſe publick things ſhould fall equally on the publick and not be made ſo many ways inconvenient to the moſt uſefull part of it, which is the Induſtrious Planter of *America*.

If it ſhould be found neceſſary to Support the *Affrican* Company for the good of the *Guinea* Trade, at the ſame time no doubt but that ſuch care will be taken of the Collonies, that they ſhall be better and cheaper ſupply'd than they have been yet, Therefore with Submiſſion to the better Underſtandings of others among the many ways that may be thought convenient, I do humbly propoſe, that any Planters may have them Delivered by Lots at a Moderate price in the Collonies, or that any Planter or Merchant giving good Security for the Payment of their Money in *England* at a certain time, may have *Negro's* at a certain Moderate profit to the *Affrican Company*, put on board their Ship at *Guinea*, or may have goods of the *Affrican* Company at a reaſonable profit to be pay'd in *England* at the return of the Ship; Or that they may have liberty to go and Trade thither, paying a moderate Sum *Per Cent.* for leave to carry their own Goods: For it is to be underſtood, that whatſoever Burthen is put upon the *Negro* Trade, the Planter pays it, and it will ſo much leſſen the Increaſe of the Plantations.

And ſince by no diſcerning perſon it can be denied but that the
Sugar

Sugar and *Tobacco-Collonies* are of very great advantage to *England*, it is not to be question'd but that our *Legiflators* will think it worth their while to Methodize that *Commerce* to the beft advantage, and to fuffer no hardfhip to be put upon the Planter, that they may be enabled to fell their Commodities in Forreign Markets, with the benefit of which to *England* will be quickly feen, and in a few years (is eafily to be demonftrated) that they will bear out all Nations that pretends to produce the like Commodities; and then a moderate Duty may be laid on their product for the Forreigners to pay, which will make Forreigners help to fupport the Charge of the Nation, and no way hurtfull to the Planter; by what has been faid for the *Sugar* and *Tobacco-Collonies*, may be faid for all *Collonies* that produces the *Commodities* of Forreign Nations, as Silk, Wines, Oyls, &c. and any other number of men that will engage to Plant and produce in fuch a Term of Years fuch a quantity of Commodities that are *Forregn Commodities*, and not already produc'd in our *Collonies*, ought to be encouraged by this Nation: For no Trade can be fo advantageous to this Nation, for the Increafing of Navigation, and the Confuming of our Wollen-Manufacture, and indeed every thing that is made or ufed in *England*, as Collonies, for they being *Englifh*, and having all their commerce from *England*, will always be initiating the Cuftomes, and Fafhions of *England*, both as to Apparell, houfhold-Furniture, Eating and Drinking, &c. For it is impoffible for them to forget from whence they come, or ever be at reft (after they have arrived to a Plentifull Eftate) untill they fettle their Families in *England*, by which means their Induftry, time and Labour is to be fpent for the Inriching the *Englifh* Nation: Further I fhall not inlarge, but leave what I have faid to the Judgement of every Judicious Reader, to amend wherein I may be defective.

FINIS.

RESEARCH LIBRARY OF COLONIAL AMERICANA

An Arno Press Collection

Histories

Acrelius, Israel. **A History of New Sweden; Or, The Settlements on the River Delaware** . . . Translated with an Introduction and Notes by William M. Reynolds. Historical Society of Pennsylvania, MEMOIRS, XI, Philadelphia, 1874.

Belknap, Jeremy. **The History of New Hampshire.** 3 vols., Vol. 1—Philadelphia, 1784 (Reprinted Boston, 1792), Vol. 2—Boston, 1791, Vol. 3—Boston, 1792.

Browne, Patrick. **The Civil and Natural History of Jamaica.** In Three Parts . . . London, 1756. Includes 1789 edition Linnaean index.

[Burke, Edmund]. **An Account of the European Settlements in America.** In Six Parts . . . London, 1777. Two volumes in one.

Chalmers, George. **An Introduction to the History of the Revolt of the American Colonies:** Being a Comprehensive View of Its Origin, Derived From the State Papers Contained in the Public Offices of Great Britain. London, 1845. Two volumes in one.

Douglass, William. **A Summary, Historical and Political, of the First Planting, Progressive Improvements, and Present State of the British Settlements in North-America.** Boston, 1749–1752. Two volumes in one.

Edwards, Bryan. **The History, Civil and Commercial, of the British Colonies in the West Indies.** Dublin, 1793–1794. Two volumes in one.

Hughes, Griffith. **The Natural History of Barbados.** In Ten Books. London, 1750.

[Franklin, Benjamin]. **An Historical Review of the Constitution and Government of Pennsylvania, From Its Origin** . . . London, 1759.

Hubbard, William. **A General History of New England, From the Discovery to MDCLXXX**. (*In* Massachusetts Historical Society, COLLECTIONS, Series 2, vol. 5, 6, 1815. Reprinted 1848.)

Hutchinson, Thomas. **The History of the Colony of Massachusetts Bay** . . . 3 vols., Boston, 1764–1828.

Keith, Sir William. **The History of the British Plantations in America** . . . London, 1738.

Long, Edward. **The History of Jamaica: Or, General Survey of the Antient and Modern State of that Island** . . . 3 vols., London, 1774.

Mather, Cotton. **Magnalia Christi Americana; Or, The Ecclesiastical History of New-England From** . . . **the Year 1620, Unto the Year** . . . **1698. In Seven Books.** London, 1702.

Mather, Increase. **A Relation of the Troubles Which Have Hapned in New-England, By Reason of the Indians There From the Year 1614 to the Year 1675** . . . Boston, 1677.

Smith, Samuel. **The History of the Colony of Nova-Caesaria, Or New-Jersey** . . . **to the Year 1721** . . . Burlington, N.J., 1765.

Thomas, Sir Dalby. **An Historical Account of the Rise and Growth of the West-India Collonies,** and of the Great Advantages They are to England, in Respect to Trade. London, 1690.

Trumbull, Benjamin. **A Complete History of Connecticut,** Civil and Ecclesiastical, From the Emigration of Its First Planters, From England, in the Year 1630, to the Year 1764; and to the Close of the Indian Wars . . . New Haven, 1818. Two volumes in one.

Personal Narratives and Promotional Literature

Byrd, William. **The Secret Diary of William Byrd of Westover, 1709–1712,** edited by Louis B. Wright and Marion Tinling. Richmond, Va., 1941.

Byrd, William. **The London Diary (1717–1721) and Other Writings,** edited by Louis B. Wright and Marion Tinling. New York, 1958.

A Genuine Narrative of the Intended Conspiracy of the Negroes at Antigua. Extracted From an Authentic Copy of a Report, Made to the Chief Governor of the Carabee Islands, by the Commissioners, or Judges Appointed to Try the Conspirators. Dublin, 1737.

Gookin, Daniel. **An Historical Account of the Doings and Sufferings of the Christian Indians in New England in the Years 1675, 1676, 1677** . . . (*In* American Antiquarian Society, Worcester, Mass. ARCHAEOLOGIA AMERICANA. TRANSACTIONS AND COLLECTIONS. Cambridge, 1836. vol. 2.)

Gookin, Daniel. **Historical Collections of the Indians in New England.** Of Their Several Nations, Numbers, Customs, Manners, Religion and Government, Before the English Planted There . . . Boston, 1792.

Morton, Thomas. **New English Canaan or New Canaan.** Containing an Abstract of New England, Composed in Three Books . . . Amsterdam, 1637.

Sewall, Samuel. **Diary of Samuel Sewall, 1674–1729.** (*In* Massachusetts Historical Society. COLLECTIONS, 5th Series, V–VII, 1878–1882.) Three volumes.

Virginia: Four Personal Narratives. (Hamor, Ralph. *A True Discourse on the Present Estate of Virginia . . . Till the 18 of June 1614* . . . London, 1615/Hariot, Thomas. *A Briefe and True Report of the New Found Land of Virginia* . . . London, 1588/Percy, George. *A Trewe Relacyon of the Proceedings and Ocurrentes of Momente Which Have Happened in Virginia From . . . 1609, Until . . . 1612.* (In *Tyler's Quarterly Historical and Genealogical Magazine*, Vol. III, 1922.)/Rolf, John. *Virginia in 1616.* (In *Virginia Historical Register and Literary Advertiser*, Vol. I, No. III, July, 1848.) New York, 1972.

Winthrop, John. **The History of New England From 1630–1649.** Edited by James Savage. Boston, 1825–1826. Two volumes in one.

New England Puritan Tracts of the Seventeenth Century

Cobbett, Thomas. **The Civil Magistrate's Power in Matters of Religion Modestly Debated** . . . London, 1653.

Cotton, John. **The Bloudy Tenent, Washed, and Made White in the Bloud of the Lambe** . . . London, 1647.

Cotton, John. **A Brief Exposition with Practical Observations Upon the Whole Book of Canticles.** London, 1655.

Cotton, John. **Christ the Fountaine of Life:** Or, Sundry Choyce Sermons on Part of the Fift Chapter of the First Epistle of St. John. London, 1651.

Cotton, John. **Two Sermons.** (*Gods Mercie Mixed with His Justice* . . . London, 1641/*The True Constitution of a Particular Visible Church, Proved by Scripture* . . . London, 1642.) New York, 1972.

Eliot, John. **The Christian Commonwealth:** Or, The Civil Policy of the Rising Kingdom of Jesus Christ. London, 1659.

Hooker, Thomas. **The Application of Redemption,** By the Effectual Work of the Word, and Spirit of Christ, for the Bringing Home of Lost Sinners to God. London, 1657.

H[ooker], T[homas]. **The Christian's Two Chiefe Lessons,** Viz. Selfe Deniall, and Selfe Tryall . . . London, 1640.

Hooker, Thomas. **A Survey of the Summe of Church-Discipline** Wherein the Way of the Churches of New England is Warranted Out of the Word, and All Exceptions of Weight, Which Are Made Against It, Answered . . . London, 1648.

Increase Mather Vs. Solomon Stoddard: Two Puritan Tracts. (Mather, Increase. *The Order of the Gospel, Professed and Practised by the Churches of Christ in New-England* . . . Boston, 1700/Stoddard, Solomon. *The Doctrine of Instituted Churches Explained, and Proved From the Word of God.* London, 1700.) New York, 1972.

Mather, Cotton. **Ratio Disciplinae Fratrum Nov-Anglorum.** A Faithful Account of the Discipline Professed and Practised, in the Churches of New England. Boston, 1726.

Mather, Richard. **Church Covenant:** Two Tracts. (*Church-Government and Church-Covenant Discussed, in an Answer to the Elders of the Severall Churches in New-England* . . . London, 1643/*An Apologie of the Churches in New-England for Church-Covenant, Or, A Discourse Touching the Covenant Between God and Men, and Especially Concerning Church-Covenant* . . . London, 1643.) New York, 1972.

The Imperial System

[Blenman, Jonathan]. **Remarks on Several Acts of Parliament Relating More Especially to the Colonies Abroad** . . . London, 1742.

British Imperialism: Three Documents. (Berkeley, George. *A Proposal for the Better Supplying of Churches in our Foreign Plantations, and for Converting the Savage Americans to Christianity by a College to be Erected in the Summer Islands, Otherwise Called the Isles of Bermuda* . . . London, 1724/[Fothergill, John]. *Considerations Relative to the North American Colonies.* London, 1765/*A Letter to a Member of Parliament Concerning the Naval-Store Bill* . . . London, 1720.) New York, 1972.

Coke, Roger. **A Discourse of Trade** . . . London, 1670.

[D'Avenant, Charles]. **An Essay Upon the Government of the English Plantations on the Continent of America** (1701). An Anonymous Virginian's Proposals for Liberty Under the British Crown, With Two Memoranda by William Byrd. Edited by Louis B. Wright. San Marino, Calif., 1945.

Dummer, Jeremiah. **A Defence of the New-England Charters** . . . London, 1721.

Gee, Joshua. **The Trade and Navigation of Great Britain Considered:** Shewing that Surest Way for a Nation to Increase in Riches, is to Prevent the Importation of Such Foreign Commodities as May Be Rais'd at Home. London, 1729.

[Little, Otis]. **The State of Trade in the Northern Colonies Considered;** With an Account of Their Produce, and a Particular Description of Nova Scotia . . . London, 1748.

Tucker, Jos[iah]. **The True Interest of Britain, Set Forth in Regard to the Colonies:** And the Only Means of Living in Peace and Harmony With Them, Including Five Different Plans for Effecting this Desirable Event . . . Philadelphia, 1776.

VSoc
HC
157
B8
T4
1972